4 Steps to a Great New Job

Change Your Stripes™

Find a job you love!

Do what you love for a living!

Second Edition

By Catherine Byers Breet

Second Edition

Copyright © 2010 Arbez™, Inc. All rights reserved.

ISBN-13 (pbk): 978-0-615-28342-5

Printed and bound in the United States of America 9 8 7 6 5 4 3 2 1

Trademarked names may appear in this book. Rather than use a trademark symbol with every occurrence of a trademarked name, we use the names only in an editorial fashion and to the benefit of the trademark owner, with no intention of infringement of the trademark.

Lead Editors: Donald J. Byers and Marj Kyriopoulos

Contributing editor: Kate Shields-Stenzinger

Cover Designer: Stefan Breet

Distributed to the book trade worldwide by Arbez™, Inc.

For information on translations, please contact Arbez™, Inc. at http://www.arbez.com.

The source code for this book is available to readers by contacting us at www.arbez.com

Dedicated to ...

all the job seekers who have asked for my help,
encouraged me to write this book,
trusted me with their stories,
and enriched my life over the years.

This book is for you.

Keep chasing those dreams!

Contents at a Glance

Table of Contents

About the Author

Catherine Byers Breet has been inspiring people to chase their dreams since she was small. She started her career working as a youth counselor for troubled teens, and her passion for helping people harness their strengths has never waned.

In 1997, Catherine unwittingly landed in the recruiting industry and has never looked back. She quickly became obsessed with helping people make the *right* career moves, not just take the first job that comes along. Thus began her toolkit of cheat sheets, tips, and tricks. Chasing her own dreams, Catherine founded Arbez™, Inc. in 2006. Her desire was to create a company where she could put as much time and energy into her candidates as she did her clients. What she has discovered is that she wants to help even more people find jobs they love.

This book is the culmination of that desire. Professionally, Catherine knows what it takes to get hired. She is a professional recruiter, motivational speaker, business owner and writer. Personally, she knows what it takes to go through a difficult job hunt. She believes that everyone deserves to be in a job they love and this book is the tool you need to do just that. Catherine lives near Minneapolis – St. Paul, MN with her husband Stefan and two sons, At and Kobus.

Acknowledgments

Writing this book has been an incredible and humbling journey. So many have been there to encourage me and shape this book; I am forever grateful for their support. I would like to take a brief moment to thank those who were particularly instrumental in helping me put this book into your hands.

I could not have walked this path without the unwavering support, inspiration and encouragement of one person: my husband, Stefan. He is *my* stripe changer. He taught me to believe in my own dreams and empowered me to go get them. As for writing this book, he simply said "You need do this. You can help many more people, and you need to do this." He would not take "No" for an answer. Thank you, Stefan. Only you know the sacrifices we've been through to make this dream a reality.

To my two sons, At and Kobus. Thank you for reminding me each and every day what life is about, inspiring me to persevere and sharing your laughter, no matter what the day.

There is a very long list of additional people whose encouragement, insight and suggestions have made this what it is. I am eternally grateful to each of them:

To my father, Donald J. Byers. Thank you for pushing me to write the very best papers I could as a small girl. Thank you for your unwavering enthusiasm and support. Lastly, thank you for your tireless editing throughout this process. To Magdaleen Breet and Oupa At Breet for embracing me, and my dreams. To Kate Shields-Stenzinger, for telling me what I have to offer the world of job seekers, and for selfless hours editing my first draft. To Marj Kyriopoulos, for a herculean editing effort at the witching hour. Your final edit was truly a gift. Wow! To my lovely sister Jennifer Frederick, for lending an ear any time of day or night, and for saying "Yes you can!" To my brother Duncan Byers, for helping me navigate the intellectual property waters.

In addition, I found inspiration and suggestions for improvement from this group of generous friends and job seekers: Anne Pryor, Cynthia Clay, Janel Woods, Jen Hanson, Kate Challeen, Kate Richards, Katherine Poindexter, Margaret McDonald, Maureen Peters, Renee Treberg and Sue Ginsburg.

Thank you for your time. Thank you for your patience. And thank you pushing me to help job seekers find work that inspires them.

Prologue

So you need a new job. You need answers to some tough questions like, "How long will it take me to find a new job?" and "Will it be the right job for me?" You want to make sure you write a resume that works and spend your time in the right places. Welcome to **Change Your Stripes™- 4 Steps to a Great New Job**, where you will get answers to all those questions, and a whole lot more. This book and companion workbook will help you get hired faster - in a job that's right for you!

This job hunt method is highly customizable. With job hunting, one size does not fit all. You are unique and you need an approach that can be tailored to who you are, what you want, and where you will find your ideal job.

Since 1997, I have been in the recruiting business, working with people as they look for new jobs. I am passionate about helping people chase their dreams, get hired faster, and do what they love for a living. I wrote this book to help more people do just that - to help job seekers get hired faster, in a job that's right for them.

Why Change Your Stripes™?

The "*Change Your Stripes*" theme is in recognition that change is everywhere; it is the one thing in life that you can count on always being there. Changing jobs means huge change. I am here to help you drive that change, so that you will get what you want in your next job.

This book is your guide to getting hired faster and easier, in a job that's right for you. It will take you all the way from "I need a new job." to "Wow, I love my new job!"

Here is your first insider tip:

The more you focus on what you want, the faster you'll get hired

You probably find that hard to believe, but I know it is true. Since 1997, I have watched countless people get hired (and not hired), and I can tell you this: the clearer you are on what you want, and the more specific you can be about it, the faster and more easily you will get a new job. In fact, a quick look at recruiter success ratios demonstrates this clearly; a recruiter can increase his success ratio, on average, from 20% to 78% simply by spending more time focusing on a candidate's drivers and motivators, and by submitting only the candidates who are a great fit for all aspects of the job and company. The same is true for job seeker job hunt success. If you spend less time chasing down the "maybe I would like this" or "maybe I am a fit for this," and focus your time and attention on the positions that make you say "Wow! This sounds like a great fit for me because of A, B and C." You will get hired faster, and land in a job you'll love doing.

If you need a job right now, you might think you don't have time to waste dreaming about what you want. You just want a job.

I argue this: if you need a job right now, you especially need to focus on what you want, because you don't have time to waste spinning your wheels in the wrong direction. Once you zero in on what you want, you will do **less work** and find a **better job,—faster!**

Here is your second insider tip:

The smarter you are about *how* you look for a new job, the faster you'll get hired

What does this mean? This means that most people struggle to find a new job because they do not know what steps to take, in what order. With *4 Steps to a Great New Job*, you'll know exactly **what to do** to go get a great new job. This book will cut through the clutter and give you quick access to the tips, tricks, and resources you need to find a job quickly. It will tell you what matters most. Most importantly, it will tell you **what steps you need to take, in what order,** to get what you want.

You may think employers have all the power in the hiring process. They don't. I will tell you what you can control in your search for a new job, as well as specific things *you can do* to gain and keep control during your job search.

Changing jobs is a wonderful opportunity to grab the life you want. Once you get started, you will be amazed to learn that you **can** have what you want in your next job.

Welcome to *Change Your Stripes*™*- 4 Steps to a Great New Job*. My sincere hope is that you will find the tools, inspiration, and guidance you need to land a job you'll love.

Now, go *Change Your Stripes*!

Why I Wrote This Book

I wrote this book because I believe everyone deserves to love what he or she does for a living. I also know that with the right tools and a bit of inspiration, you can get a job you love. I was tired of seeing good people struggle to find good jobs and I knew I could offer a simple process, along with some tools and inspiration, to help them get what they want and deserve in a job. Traditionally, people have gone to career coaches to get this type of assistance. Career coaches are wonderful, but they are financially out of reach for most job seekers.

According to a recent survey by Careerbuilder.com, 84% of American workers are dissatisfied with their jobs. I think that is unacceptable and I intend to change it!

I love recruiting, but I have had one enormous frustration over the years—I could not help everyone I met find a new job. I had the knowledge and ability to do so, but it was impossible for me to offer one-on-one coaching to all of them. As a recruiter, my job was to focus on finding candidates to fill open positions.

In fact, a manager who saw me trying to help a candidate who was obviously not a fit for our company said to me, "We are not the Red Cross." That burned me at the time, and it still burns when I think about it. On the one hand, he was right to reprimand me. We were paid to hire people who qualified for open positions and if I personally coached every candidate I touched, I would never be successful. On the other hand, on that day, I realized that I had to find a way to do both—fill jobs **and** help everyone I met during the course of a day.

Since then, I have been looking for a way to support everyone I meet who is looking for a new job. I tried to find a place where I could refer people who said to me, "I know I'm not a fit your open positions, but can you help me? Can you recommend a book or a web site where I can get the help I need? I don't know if I am doing what I need to do to get a new job. I go to the Internet and get overwhelmed with information. What do I need to know?" I kept looking for a solution, but was unable to find it.

One day, the answer came to me: "*You* build it for them!" So, I have done just that. I captured my own time-tested 4-step job hunt process, passion, and knowledge for you here. This book was designed to give you information, inspiration and a proven method with actionable steps for getting hired faster and easier.

How to Use this Book and Workbook

Here are some tips on how to use *Change Your Stripes™- 4 Steps to a Great New Job*. Number one, start at the beginning. Read this book from cover to cover before you start the workbook—and before you continue your job search. It is a quick read, and well worth your time. You need to understand the big picture before jumping in.

If you have already put some of the pieces together (like, you already know what you want and who your target market is), that's fantastic! You can check those off and move to the next section. Just make sure not to jump in at the middle. The real value of this book and workbook is in understanding the process—**taking the right steps in the right order**.

What to Expect

The 4-Step Process:

I've taken the guesswork out of what you need to do to get a great new job. I've wrapped my arms around the process of looking for a new job and broken it into bite-sized steps. Stop asking yourself, "Am I doing the right things to get a new job?" You *are* doing the right things if you follow this simple, 4-step process.

The Book:

This book is designed to help you execute the 4-step process and customize your job search. It's packed with insight and stories that illustrate each concept I introduce.

The Worksheets:

It's one thing to say, "Know what you want" and, "Be smart about where and how you look for a job." However, the next smart question is, "How?"

In the workbook, you will find practical exercises and templates to help you define what you want in your next job, identify your target market, and create your resume, cover letter, and other key elements of your job search.

Set the Stage for Success

Before you jump into your job search, you need to set the stage for success. That means taking care of some things at home and identifying your support network. A great way to minimize frustration and ensure success while job hunting is to set up an island, or "safe zone" where you can regroup and get back on track. I've put together some suggestions on how to do that. They are as follows:

Stop.

Just stop!

How many times in life have you jumped in to something only to kick yourself later and say "Why didn't I think about this before I started? Why didn't I make a plan?" Job hunting is no different.

Just breathe! Don't forget to breathe. Today. Tomorrow. As you shake a hand and introduce yourself at a networking event. Right before a job interview. Anytime your nerves start to get the best of you.

Whether you got here on your own or with the help of someone else, you've decided that you need a new job. If you have been here before, you already know that this is going to be hard work. If this is your first search for a new job, you are likely still stunned and afraid of what awaits you on this journey. You need to acknowledge that. Changing jobs is high on the list of stressors in life. So, before you jump into solution mode, stop and do something nice for yourself. Recognize that this is tough stuff. Be gentle with yourself. **You will find a great new job.**

Now, go blow off steam doing something fun. Find a fun outlet. A friend of mine who was laid off decided to go bowling. She bowled a lot. Throwing bowling balls down the lane, watching the pins get slammed into the gutter, helped her get rid of some of the anger and frustration she felt. Physical activity is a great way to let off steam. Even a simple walk can make a world of difference in the way you feel.

In short, whenever you are feeling overwhelmed during your search for a new job, just stop, take a break, and go do something nice for yourself.

Protect Yourself

If you are about to lose your job, or if you just lost your job, you need to take some steps to protect your finances and your health. I'll offer some quick tips on how to do that. Of course, everybody's situation is unique, but there are some primary issues that arise when changing jobs. Be proactive so you don't have to worry about these things while you are focused on getting a new job. Once you take care of these things, you will be able to focus your time and attention on your job hunt and not get distracted with worry over these other issues. Here are some things to consider immediately:

Finances

- **Understand your investments:** Do not immediately withdraw cash out of your 401K plan! Take time to understand your options and make choices that are best for you and your family—short term and long term.

- **Manage your budget:** Make a household budget. Know how much money you have, where you can spend it, and where and when you can trim expenses to minimize your stress during your job search.

- **Make a plan:** How will you cover expenses if it takes you 3-6 months or longer to find a job? If you may not be able to pay your bills, consider consulting with a financial professional now. The sooner you make a plan, the easier it will be to breathe and focus on your job search.

- **Get assistance:** Find out if you qualify for unemployment insurance or a severance package at your former employer

Insurance

Insurance is something to consider. The biggest one to consider is healthcare. You should also take a look at some peripheral insurance coverage that many employers offer, such as short and long-term disability, as well as life insurance. My biggest advice is to do some research and make sure that you and family are covered, yet that you are not paying more than you need to be for that coverage.

- **Healthcare:** What is available through your former employer? Will you qualify for state healthcare coverage? Can you go onto a spouse's healthcare coverage?

  The Consolidated Omnibus Budget Reconciliation Act (COBRA) gives workers and their families who lose their health benefits the right to continue group health benefits provided by their group health plan for limited periods of time under certain circumstances (such as voluntary or involuntary job loss, reduction in the hours worked, transition between jobs, death, divorce, and other life events). Qualified individuals may be required to pay the entire premium for coverage up to 102 percent of the cost to the plan)

- **Life insurance:** Do you need it? Will it go away if you leave your present employer? Can you carry it forward from your employer?

- ***Note:*** *Even if you can carry it forward, this is rarely the most affordable option for you.*

Legal Considerations

Do you have any non-compete agreements with your former employer that will limit your job search? You need to know up-front what they are.

Identify Available Resources

- Are you eligible for unemployment insurance?

- Are you eligible for dislocated workers' support (through your state)?
- Are you eligible for training through the state?
- Are you eligible for any outplacement services through your employer?

In summary, make sure you think about big life issue like finances and insurance. Once you take care of these things, you will have the peace of mind to put all your energy into finding a new job.

Worksheet 01: Protect yourself

Find a Champion

There is no good reason to do this alone—and you do not have to. At minimum, choose one friend who will act as your champion, coach, and inspirer as you go out into the world and say, "Hire me!" Your champion is there to help you stay on track, to celebrate your successes, and to get you going again when you stumble. Often, this is a spouse or a best friend—someone you can turn to when you need to blow off steam and share your anger over your former employer or how you are feeling about your job search. It is critical to keep your negativity contained during your job hunt (which can be difficult sometimes) and so you need someone you can trust to be your sounding board.

Be specific when you ask someone to be your champion or coach. He or she will need to know what you want and need from them so he or she can be there for you in the right way. This is the person you can trust to let you know when you are straying from your goal—someone who will be there for you on the really tough days. Set clear expectations on both sides and plan to connect regularly for updates.

On the power of friendship: Do not underestimate the importance of having positive people to support you during your job hunt. Surround yourself with people who adore you and support you. Get rid of those who don't—at least for now (if not forever). It helps if you have friends who believe in you. Many times your champion will believe in you and your dreams, even when you have your doubts. You need that during your search for a new job.

Tips on finding a champion:

- Find a friend
- Ask that friend to be your coach, support, mirror
- Set clear expectations
- Plan regular meetings
- Don't ask for too little
- Don't ask for too much

Professionally, you can ask for support from someone who has worked alongside you. Choose someone who understands your strengths, weaknesses, and passions as they relate to your work. This is usually not someone with whom you can voice your anger and frustrations. (Save those feelings for your personal champion.) Ask this person to help you tell your professional story, remind you of what makes you great, review your resume, and to help you figure out where you'll find the job you want and need.

Do not try to do this alone. Lean on people and they will be there for you. Everything in life is easier with other people by your side. You will return the favor, so don't be afraid to ask for help. But make sure you ask.

Worksheet 02: Find a champion

How can I ask someone for this much help? I hate asking for help!

It is never easy to ask for help. But you need to do it. The sooner you ask for help, the sooner you'll find a job. One view of asking for help is this: people actually love to help. Call it the human condition. We each get tremendous satisfaction in helping others. But you have to ask to get that help. If you do not ask, most people are afraid to offer their help—afraid they may offend you by suggesting that you need help.

Yes, this is a very personal and sensitive topic. Yes, it is uncomfortable at times to ask for and get the feedback you need. But what would be worse? Getting direct and honest feedback from someone you know and trust, or getting it from some stranger in an interview, after you bungled the interview for your dream job?

What about job support groups? Are they a good place to go for support?

Yes and no. It depends on what type of support you are looking for. Job support groups are designed to:

- Help you meet new people and expand your network
- Let you tell your story—clearly and concisely
- Get new ideas on how to find a job
- Help other people in their hunt for a new job

Did you notice the last bullet point? You are there to help others as well. The more you help others, the more they will help you.

The name "job support group" can be misleading. These groups can be a great place to get information, inspiration, and make connections. However, they are not "support" groups in the way that many people envision. They are not the place to talk about the bad stuff you're feeling. Everyone there is focused on one thing: figuring out how to go get a new job. They are there to learn and, yes, to help others. People go to support groups to help each other find new jobs, not to share war stories. Even church job support groups are designed to help you move forward, not to bemoan the way you were laid off or what a tough time you are having in your job hunt. Unfortunately, lamenting about your search in this setting can be detrimental to you. Nobody will tell you that directly, but quietly, people will squirm and want to move on.

When you really need someone to talk to about how hard your week has been, a job support group is not the place to be. That is when you need your champion(s). You do need a safe and supportive place to debrief and work through your challenges and frustrations. No group setting is the place for that, unless it is a counseling group.

Remember: *When you need a pick-me-up, turn to your more intimate network to get a sympathetic ear.*

Find Your Happy Place

Food for thought: As mental attitude improves, so does confidence

During your job hunt, you need to **know how to find your smile**. I do not need to tell you that some days and moments are going to be tough. You already know that. You will need something to get yourself through the setbacks and prep you for the tough or scary phone calls and meetings. I like to call that place your "happy place."

Your champion(s) will not be there for you every minute of every day. For instance, when you are about to walk into an interview, you need something to ground you, to get you over your anxiety and into your strong zone. Find something that makes you happy, that eases the tension. For some of you, it might be a picture of your kids. For others, it might be your favorite music or a motivational speaker you listen to in your car.

Hot Tip: Get a little brag book

It is a great idea to get a little brag book you can use to write down your small wins. Yes, a little diary to capture the small successes and big wins during your search for a new job. Learn to see and celebrate the little things. This may sound silly, but it really works. On those tough days when you are feeling discouraged and deflated, you can pull out your little brag book and remind yourself of all the positive things that are happening in your job hunt.

Here are some sample brag book entries from people looking for a new job:

5-8: Made it through first money conversation (about salary) without stumbling! I stated clearly and concisely to the recruiter at ABC Company what I wanted for compensation and then shut up and let him talk. It was great! He did not blink and said that what I wanted was on the higher end of their range, but definitely something they could work with.

5-12: I made a cold call to XYZ Inc. (called the Chief Financial Officer) and she called me back the next day! She took 10 minutes to listen to what I wanted and referred me to another person inside the company. Yee-hah! I was petrified to make the call, but look what happened when I picked up the phone!

5-15: Five people returned my calls this week!

5-17: I went to one of those networking groups. I was terrified, but I went anyway, and made two great new connections. I am going to meet them both for coffee to network more!

5-25: I made 20 calls every day this week. Consistently! The first five made me want to throw up, but after that they got much easier.

5-26: The VP of IT at 123Company told me I have a fantastic message (my 30-second pitch about who I am and how I can add value), and while they cannot hire me right now, he knows two people he wants to connect me with. Yippee!

Now, go find the little things that will pick you up on the bad days and inspire you to face the challenges.

Notify Friends and Colleagues

If you have just lost your job, there are probably some people you'll want to notify right away. If you are going to quit your job, you'll want to think about who to notify and how. It can be tricky to notify colleagues, so take some time to think about the right way to let others know. You need to quit with your boss first and let others know about it second.

Yes, you can wait! But if you want to let people know, here are some tips on how to do it:

Family and friends: Let your close network know immediately. Chances are, you occasionally receive personal emails and calls at work. You don't want your family and friends to call your old work number. Send a quick email letting people know that you are no longer with that company and give them your new contact details. Then, follow up with phone calls. If you are not sure what to tell people, just keep it simple. When they ask you "What do you want to do next? How can I help?" say, "Thank you so much for offering. This is new (if it is) and I have not had a chance to sit down and make a plan yet. Once I do, I'll be sure to share it with you."

No matter how angry or bruised you are (if you got laid off, for instance), keep the message simple and positive. Practice if you have to. Do not send out negative messages, as it will only hurt you in the long run.

Professional acquaintances: Make a list of the business people who should know about the change. You want them to know you are leaving and you also want their help finding something new. If they don't know, they can't help you.

Understand How and Why You Got Here

It is important for you to understand how and why you got here. Whether you are still employed and just considering a move or you got laid off (or even fired), you need to be honest with yourself and figure out why you are here. This is the first step to taking control of your career—and your job hunt. Even if you are here through no fault of your own (company layoff, merger, bankruptcy), it is important to understand the path that led you there and what that means for you in the future.

The three primary reasons you need to start thinking about how you got here:

1 **For your own well being—today and tomorrow.**
Understanding what brought you here will help you avoid it, or prepare for it, next time around. This is especially important if you are sitting here wondering what on earth just happened to you. It is possible that you could not have seen this coming. Even that is powerful knowledge. Imagine how freeing it is, emotionally, to know that there was nothing you could have done to prevent this. What if the answer is as simple as this? "I was in the wrong job!"

2 **So you choose a better job next time, if there is something you want to avoid.**

3 People (networking with you and interviewing you) will want to know.
Be prepared to answer questions about why you left your prior companies. Recruiters and hiring managers will push for detail. If you can explain it quickly and easily, the conversation will move on. If you stumble and fall, struggling to explain it, you will raise concerns and get stuck on it. Everyone knows that bad things happen to good people. What they want to know is this: Did you learn from it, will you see it coming next time around, and will you know what to do about it?

How did you get here and what can you learn from it?

It might take you some time to really understand, honestly, how you got here. But you need to do it. You need to start seeing the red flags in your career before they knock you over. Name the reasons you got to this stage because, if they remain the elephant in the room, they will become barriers to your success in your job hunt. We will talk later about fear in your job hunt, and ways to overcome your fears. Very often, there are pieces in your past that are haunting you. We want to crush those fears and free you to go get what you want in your next job.

There is no shame in being unemployed! According to a recent government survey, the average American will change jobs at least 10 times in a lifetime. So you are not alone. I challenge you to find someone who has not changed jobs, and send that person to me so I can help them prepare for it.

Here are some common reasons people start looking for a new job. Which one(s) best describe you?

- **I got laid off**
- **I got fired**
- **The job**
  - o I hate my job
  - o I do not have the tools or resources I need
  - o I am bored
  - o There is no training when I need it
- **Company leadership/vision**
  - o I hate my boss
  - o I cannot see where the company is going
  - o Priorities are constantly shifting
  - o I am not a part of the company's strategy and vision
  - o Communication is unreliable or nonexistent
- **The company culture**
  - o I am not appreciated or recognized
  - o I cannot see career growth opportunities
  - o There is no teamwork or collaboration
- **Compensation**
  - o I feel I am underpaid
  - o There is a salary freeze
  - o My company has a 3% cap on salary increases
- **Perceived or real company instability**
  - o I am concerned about a lay-off
  - o My job is going away (merger/downsizing)

Going through this exercise may uncover some real challenges for you to think about. In **"Name Your Fears,"** you can work through these challenges and learn about appropriate ways to handle them. For instance, if you have been laid off twice in the last three years, you may be terrified about explaining it. In this section, I share a story about someone who had to handle that very fear.

If you got laid off, **it is not your fault.** So let go of your shame around that. Layoffs are extremely common, and they dig deep into the fabric of talented employees. It is a rare person who will not experience a layoff in his or her career.

If you got fired, listen carefully to me. **You were in the wrong job.** People do not get fired from jobs they love. They get fired from jobs that are a really bad fit for them. Then, rather than quit when they should, they stay and try to make it work and end up either outright misbehaving or taking a slow and painful road to getting fired.

Remember: The more you pay attention to who you are and what you want, the faster you'll get hired. So do not avoid this tough stuff. The sooner you can identify these things and figure out to handle them, the sooner you will remove them as barriers to your job hunt success.

Moving forward, we'll take a close look at company culture, job duties, and other "happiness at work" factors to make sure you pick a job that is right for you. Start thinking about what a great company culture would be for you and how you will know it when you see it. "Great company culture" needs to be high on your list of must-haves (coming up in **STEP 1: Know What You Want**). Once you start preparing for interviews, you will develop questions (with my help) to uncover a company's real culture.

Now that you have identified what has brought you here, pay attention to those things as you move through this process, and as you look for a new job.

Okay! You are now ready to get started on your hunt for a terrific new job. Let's go!

The Change Your Stripes™ 4-Step Process

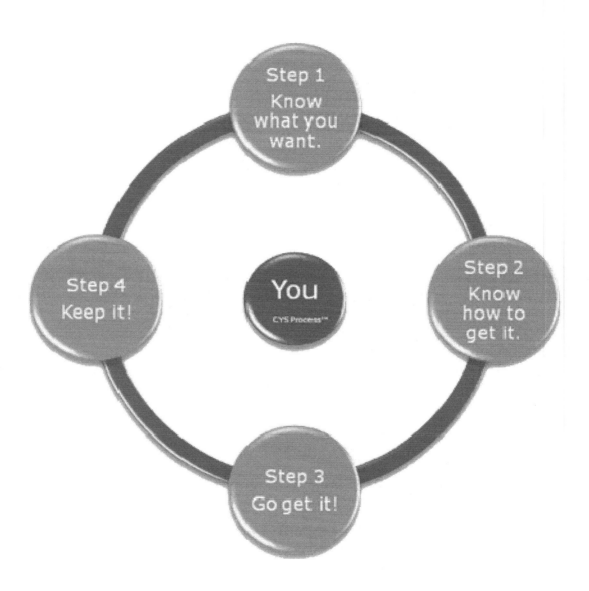

The Change Your Stripes™ 4-Step Process Detail

- Know what you want
- Know what you don't want
- Know what you need
- Name your fears

- Identify your target market
- Tell a compelling story (resume, cover letter, 30-second pitch)
- Make a plan

- Go yell it from the mountain
- Find the jobs
- Network for success
- Interview with a bang
- Get the job that's right for you

- Go yell it from the mountain (Take 2)
- Launch for success
- Pay it forward
- Keep your network alive
- Keep dreaming

STEP 1: Know What You Want

"It is essential to know yourself before you decide what work you want to do."

—Dr. Stephen R. Covey, *The 8th Habit*

The **single most important part of getting a job is this: know what you want**. Once you know clearly what you want, you will be amazed at how much easier your job hunt will be. Everything will be easier—knowing where to look and who to talk to, presenting yourself in interviews, and negotiating for and getting what you want.

Jumping headlong into a job hunt before you figure this out is like jumping into a river without a boat. Sure, you will reach your destination, but do you really want to work that hard?

Remember: *The more you focus on what you want in your next job, the faster you'll get hired.*

According to Richard Nelson Bolles in *What Color is your Parachute*, taking this approach will give you an 86% better chance of finding a new job than other methods (like mailing out resumes, for example, which will give you a 7% return on your investment).

The truth is that most job seekers, no matter how talented or articulate, are not clear on what they want, and are unable to tell other people what they want. The tragedy is that very few job seekers are aware of this gap. When I ask people if they have trouble describing what they want, most of them say "No." Yet, when these same people describe to me what they want, I have trouble understanding them. Telling people "I am really open" or "I will look at any jobs" will not help you find a job. In fact, it will hurt you. Who knows what to do with that piece of information? How can someone help you? They can't.

When I work with people who are struggling in their job hunt, nine times out of 10, this is the biggest thing standing in the way. Once they fix this, everything gets much easier.

If you can't tell people what you want, specifically, that issue will stand in the way of you getting any job—let alone a job you'll love.

Before you dismiss this chapter and say, "I know what I want and other people know what I want," sit with this for a little bit. Are you sure that other people understand what you want? Some of you can see it and taste it. That is great! But can other people see what you see? Often, they speak a different language (manager versus director, marketing versus sales, account management versus sales) and live in a very different world than you do. So you must tell them what you want in a language **they** can understand, internalize, and take to the streets for you. So please, even if you think you know clearly what you want, run through this chapter. You may be surprised what you discover.

Let's take a look at two examples:

Joe's story

Joe's desired job: waiter

Joe wants a new job as a waiter. At a networking event, this is what he says to people he meets:

> "Hi. My name is Joe. I am unemployed and am looking or a new job as a waiter. I'll work anywhere, but I live in Burnsville, so south of the cities would be great. Can you help me?"

Meet Joe's competition: Mike.

Mike also wants a job as a waiter, and he is at the same networking event. Here is how he introduces himself:

> "Hi. My name is Mike Smith. What brings you here today?"

> "I am looking for a new job as a waiter at an upscale metro restaurant. I study wines in my spare time and hope to open my own restaurant by the age of 40. I am looking for networking contacts like restaurant owners or liquor distributors who sell to restaurants. Oh, and I love adventure travel, so if you know of anyone looking to plan a great vacation, I can help. How can I help you today?"

Both Joe and Mike want a new job as a waiter. Who do you think will get more job leads? Who do you think people will go out of their way to help? Mike, of course, and here is why:

He is confident. He is clear about what he wants. He gives people something they can sink their teeth into. He does not put limitations on where he will work in his first conversation. Nor does he mention that he just got laid off. Of course he will share that information if someone asks, but he doesn't share it up front: too much information.

The truth is, Mike will consider a job at any restaurant, but he really wants to find one at an upscale restaurant. He needs a job really quickly. So why is Mike better off telling people "upscale restaurants" rather than just "any restaurant?" Well, it is easier for you to think of restaurants, and people you know at restaurants, if he is specific about what he wants.

If I met Mike at a networking event, I would refer him to a friend of mine who imports wines. Guess who my friend sells to and knows well? Owners of fine restaurants around town. The "adventure travel" reference is something unique to share. It will help people remember Mike. It is fun and interesting to share. Lastly, Mike asked, "How can I help you?" That is the fastest way to turn an initial meeting into a meaningful one. From "I need a new red wagon for my son" to "I am actually looking for a new job, too," you simply cannot go wrong by asking how you can help someone else.

Michele's story:

Michele wants a technology sales job. She has worked in technology sales for 10 years, loves it, and is good at it. She was a top performer at her last company. She was just laid off and is confident she will land a new job easily. Sounds simple enough. Right? Wrong. Here is why:

Michele believes she will land a job quickly (which she will) and loves meeting people, so she is going out fearlessly networking, networking, networking. All great stuff. Here is the problem: she is working harder than she needs to, and, as a result, she's stalling her job hunt because she is not telling people **clearly and concisely** what she wants. When she meets Jim, she says, "Hi, Jim. My name is Michele Jones. I am looking for a job in IT sales. Do you happen to know anyone I can talk to?"

What is wrong with what she is saying? First, it is too general—especially since Jim knows nothing about IT sales (he is a finance guy). Jim doesn't know of any immediate IT job openings. He doesn't even understand IT, so he quickly ends the conversation with, "Oh, okay. I'll keep you in mind." They smile, shake hands, and Michele leaves thinking, "Great. Jim will call me if he hears about any opportunities." Here is the problem: Jim might remember Michele, but he probably won't remember what she does beyond "sales." Furthermore, his neighbor might tell him about a job opening that is perfect for her (like a business development position at a software development firm), but won't think of her because she did not tell him what she really wants.

If Michele had given more specific information, the connections would start happening much faster. Let's see what happens if Michele tries a more targeted approach:

"Hi, my name is Michele Jones. I have been selling software since 1998 and love it (software like Oracle and PeopleSoft). Have you heard of those packages? I am on the hunt for a new job in software product sales and would love to talk to anyone who works at software development companies likes ABC Corp. or TTT Inc. Do you happen to know anyone at companies like these who might be open to networking with me?"

If Michele frames what she does in terms anyone can understand, dropping company names, connections start to click. Jim suddenly thinks of his friend who works at ABC Corp. and he gives Michele his name. Furthermore, he now has an understanding of what she does and is more likely to remember her when he hears his neighbor, CEO at a company, say "job opening" and "software development experience." Let's assume the job opening is in marketing, not sales. That's okay. Here is what will likely happen: Jim will say to his neighbor "I don't know of a marketing candidate for you, but I do know a software sales person, and I'll bet Michele might have some candidates for you." This is how the network expands. And the CEO might just have an open sales position as well.

If you do already know, clearly, what you want, that is fantastic! Move on to **Worksheet 11: What I want** and write it down. If you have any hesitation about what you want, you'll want to read on to get a clearer sense of what you want.

Throughout this process of self-discovery, you must be honest with yourself. The clearer you are about where you have been and where you want to go, the easier it will be. This is not about what other people want. This is about who you are, where you are at your best, and what you want. Perhaps friends are pushing you to go for a management job because you are good at it and it pays well. Yet, in your heart, you really do not want to manage people anymore. Be honest with yourself about that. If you go for the management job anyway because other people think you should, you will not be happy there. Worse, you may not be very successful in that role, largely because your heart is not in it. That is a vicious cycle to get trapped in. So stop the madness! Follow your heart.

Take some time and make sure your instinct is right

Unless you spend some time on this, you might jump to conclusions that are entirely wrong about what motivates you and what you want. Then, you may wake up six months later in a job you do not like. Do not let that happen to you! Take some time now, up front, to pin it down. I promise, it will pay off.

Barry's story:

> Meet Barry. When he first started his job hunt, he thought he knew what he wanted—a technology leadership job at a small or medium-sized software development company. When I first asked him why he wanted this, he said he wanted to work on a leading-edge product (first of its kind on the market). He was certain that a really neat, exciting product was most important to him. He really believed that would make him happy at work.

> When I dug deeper into Barry's past jobs and put him through a few workbook exercises, Barry discovered that it is actually the *process* of developing a great product and knowing that the product is *high quality* that gets him jumping out of bed in the morning. He did not have to be on the leading edge of technology. He loved building high-quality products (well-designed and delivered). After working for a software development firm that did not value quality and pushed products out the door before they were market-ready, he realized how much he hated working there. He was not proud of the product and was constantly fighting fires after product launch. That frustrated his team and demoralized them as well. This is a slightly different twist, but an important one. He is now asking very different questions during the interview process and has opened himself up to many more companies than he initially thought.

Knowing what you want is not only important in making connections. It is important in every aspect of your job hunt—writing a resume that works, networking, searching for jobs in the right places, and interviewing well. And it goes without saying, of course, that the more you know what you want, the much better your chances of getting it.

So, if you take away only one message from this book, I want it to be this one:

The more you focus on what you want, the faster you'll get hired.

As you move through this chapter, here are some questions that may arise.

"Why can't I just figure out what I want as I go along? I am really open to all possibilities."

Well, you probably are open to possibilities. However, that does not preclude you from telling people what you want in specific terms they can understand. This is a tough concept to get across, so bear with me as I try to explain. Let's think about Joe and Mike (the waiters) again. Mike will work anywhere right now, because he needs to pay his bills. However, he gives people a limited view (clear and concise) of what he wants because it will help him network and he also knows he would enjoy working at an upscale restaurant. There are many reasons why taking this leap and turning what you want into a simple list people can understand is worth your time.

The most important reasons are:

- You will waste a lot less time in the wrong places.
- You will get closer to what you want if you are clear about what you want.
- People who *want* to help you will be able to do so.
- You, and what makes you happy, will not get lost in this job hunt process.

If you are open to possibilities, that is wonderful—and you should be! You should consider new and interesting possibilities. There is a difference between being open to possibilities and conducting an effective job hunt. In order to conduct an effective job hunt, you need to pin down at bare minimum things you want and tailor your search so you don't waste time, and so others are able to understand how to help you.

Here is the problem with being totally open: You will be wandering all over the place and you can waste a lot of time on jobs you ultimately do not want to do. Also, people will not know how to help you very much if you say "I am totally open; I will do anything." They will love your enthusiasm (as do I), but they will not know where to direct you. Often, once people take this first step and actually name what it is that they want, it actually opens up possibilities for them. Their job search becomes broader (new industries, new roles) and yet still much easier.

I could talk for ages about people I know who jumped headlong into their job search without asking themselves "what do I really want?" They wasted time, they shed tears, and they landed in jobs they hated. **Do not let that be you!**

When you want to go on vacation, do you walk into a travel agency, hand them your credit card and say, "Send me anywhere! I don't care"? When shopping for a new house, would you say to a realtor, "Show me anything in my budget—any neighborhood, any size, any style"? (No realtor would let you send them off on a wild goose chase like that either, because they know it is a tremendous waste of time). So why would you do that in your search for a new job? Because you did not know you were doing it! Now you *do* know better, and now you have the tools you need to work much smarter in your job hunt.

If you are already in the middle of your job search, do not despair. This 4-step process and set of workbook exercises will help you quickly get back on track. It will also give you a number of "ah-hah" moments to shed light on why things have been so difficult for you at various stages.

"How can I figure out what I want?"

This entire chapter, *STEP 1: Know What You Want* will help you figure out what you want. Like all important decisions in life, you need to take some time to think about this.

You may have never really explored what you want and why you want those things. I will help you with this. I have developed a program and a set of worksheets to help you identify your dreams and key happiness factors at work. This is not just about getting a job. It is about getting a job that is right for *you*. Discover what makes you love and hate work, and then turn that knowledge into a wish list for your future.

First, you are going to dream big! Get back in touch with what you wanted when you were young, before responsibility started getting in the way of doing everything you wanted. Think first about the *life* you want, not the *job* you want. When you were ten years old, what did you dream of doing with your life? When you were fifteen? Twenty? What would you do if you won the lotto tomorrow and did not have to work another day in your life?

Second, you will walk through your past jobs, and flesh out what you loved about them, what you hated about them and how well they fit your passion and desires.

Third, you will use **Worksheet 11: What I want** and **Worksheet 10: My non-negotiables** to commit what you want to paper

Fourth, you will begin to identify which jobs can give you what you want in life. With **Worksheet 12: My perfect job,** you will start to see and taste the job you'll love. Last, with **Worksheet 13: Identify the gaps**, you will pinpoint the skills and experiences you need to go get that dream job (to determine whether or not you have what it takes to get your dream job today). Most of you will be able to get that dream job right now with better self-branding and clearer communication. A few of you, however, will realize that your dream job requires further education or experience. That is perfectly fine! Once you know this, it will be easy to take a straight path toward your perfect job.

Not sure what you want?

Not sure what you want? That's okay! As I said earlier, very few people do. We run at a furious pace. Few of us have really thought about what we want in our career. Now is your chance. Stop taking whatever comes your way and drive the career you want, not what everyone else wants. These next few sections will help you rediscover your passion and uncover what you really want from work.

Remember Your Dreams

Children know how to dream shamelessly. They also stay true to what they love doing. When you ask a child if he wants to take piano lessons, he is not afraid to say "No! I don't!" When you ask him what he wants to be when he grows up, he usually answers, with some ambitious expectations, "Superhero." "Astronaut." "Rock star." "President of the United States." There is beauty and truth in his innocent and heartfelt answers.

So what happens to those childhood dreams? Why do so few people go chase their dreams? Why is there only one Tiger Woods? Kids begin to realize that there are mountains to climb, and naysayers in their midst. It *is* a lot of work to become an astronaut or a doctor or the President of the United States. Adults start to put barriers in front of them like, "We don't have the money to send you to college." "It takes years of schooling before you can become a doctor. Do you really want to work that hard?" "A rock star? Are you serious? What makes you think *you* have what it takes to be a rock star? Have you seen how good those other kids are?" "A superhero? There is no such thing."

Is that really true? There may not be a Spiderman, but there are certainly people who do some pretty super heroic things for a living, like firefighters, soldiers, brain surgeons.

Worse than the barriers adults put in front of children are the barriers they put in front of themselves. I met an artist who works with elementary school children the other day and we got talking about childhood dreams. She said that, by the time a child is in fifth grade, many children have already started giving up on their dreams. When she asks kindergarteners "Who here is an artist?" they all raise their hands. When she asks fifth graders the same question, only a few raise their hands. Self-doubt and public reinforcement of that doubt get to us at a very early age.

A year later, I watched this unfolding with my own son, before my very eyes. He is a gifted artist. Truly. From sketching to painting to creating wildlife scenes with cutouts, he does some amazing artwork. He loves it. He actually said to me one day "Doing art energizes me." Wow. He is six and in first grade. I am, of course, delighted to see that he has found something that makes him happy. And yet, just a few weeks ago, in first grade, he came home in tears one day and said "I'm not an artist!" When I said "What do you mean?" he replied "The other kids laughed at my painting today and said it is no good. I don't want to do art anymore." You can imagine my surprise. Already? In First Grade? Yes, I am afraid so.

Who took away *your* dreams? Are you ready to go get them back? I know you can! I have watched countless people take control of their destiny, chase their dreams, and accomplish incredible things. Dream big. Go for the gold. You deserve to love what you do for a living.

My story, as an illustration:

When I was a kid, I wanted to be a National Geographic Photojournalist.

Why?

- World Travel
- Discovering other cultures, different people
- Helping people tell their unique stories
- Writing
- Photography

Did I become what I dreamed about becoming? At first blush ... no. Not at all. But if you look a little closer, you'll see that I did get some of what I wanted, despite myself. I have traveled to six countries. I meet new and interesting people in my job every day. I get to help people tell their career stories in the context of their careers every day. I am a writer. I am an avid hobby photographer. And now that I have realized clearly and concisely what gets me jumping out of bed in the morning, it is much easier for me to hold onto that and stay focused on work that I love doing.

I still think I would have loved that job as a photojournalist. I still devour magazines about world travel and travel abroad whenever I can. So what happened to me? Why didn't I become a photojournalist? I distinctly remember feeling as a teenager that I would never be good enough to work for National Geographic. I thought I was not good enough. I thought I needed a lot of money for school and travel to realize that dream. I decided I should go for something less ambitious, and try to get a summer job overseas. I thought "I have college loans I need to pay off. I need to hunker down and pay off those loans. Then I'll figure out how to see the world."

Today, I believe I actually did chase those dreams over the years by many of the choices I made—but only halfway. You never will be top of your game, able to compete with the best of breed, if you do not commit your heart and soul. I worked summer jobs away from home. I travel overseas when I can. But I never gave it the focus and gusto to actually become a photojournalist. **What if** I had believed in my dreams as a little girl? **What if** I had not started seeing barriers in front of me?

So, go remember your dreams. Commit them to paper. It's the only way you are going to get what you want. Once you do that, you *can* get your dream job! You *can* love what you do for a living! You will have to chart a deliberate course, and perhaps get more education or experience, but your dream job is yours to have. You are working hard to find a job already. Why not work a little smarter and get a job that's right for you while you're at it?

Go do the following worksheets:

Worksheet 03: When I was a kid . . .

Worksheet 04: Other people thought I would become . . .

Worksheet 05: Did you chase your dreams?

Recapture Your Passion

"Your power to choose the direction of your life allows you to reinvent yourself, to change your future, and to powerfully influence the rest of what you create."

—Dr. Stephen R. Covey

Where is your passion in life? Your dream job is all about doing what you love, not working to pay the bills. You are here because you want that in life. Where do you find the fire in your belly and a twinkle in your eyes? Some say this is their calling. Others say it is what gets them jumping out of bed on the day they get to do it. What do *you* love doing? Solving problems? Helping others? Empowering others? Putting the pieces together? If all you can come up with is a broad activity, try to dig in to precisely what you enjoy about that activity. For example, if you honestly love gardening, what do you love about gardening? You may discover that it is the planning, the planting, the nurturing, seeing the fruits of your labor. Certainly you love the feel of the dirt on your hands, but it is possible that you can find that type of enjoyment at a desk job. Planning, planting seeds (in people or processes), and watching your ideas grow. Or, perhaps it really is the great outdoors you love. If that is the case, then the world is your oyster and your dream job might be something entirely different than gardening.

Go do the following worksheet:

Worksheet 06: My passion in life

Remember the Fun at Work

Now tap into the fun you've had at work over the years. Undoubtedly, there will be patterns and similarities over the years in what you loved doing. Once you identify these, they will point to what you do well and what you want to do next. The more you understand your "happy factors" and write them down on paper, the clearer your passions and desires will become. Now go recapture that fire by using these worksheets:

Worksheet 07: My favorite job as a teenager

Worksheet 08: My favorite job as an adult

Know What You Do Not Want

Now that you've had a fun walk down memory lane, it's time to take a look at the dark times in your career and the job(s), or aspects of your jobs, you hated. Perhaps knowing what you do **not** want is more important than knowing what you want. I call these your "non-negotiables." They are the things that you should not compromise on when looking for a new job. It is important to commit them to paper and stick to them. It will make it easier to avoid wasting time during your job hunt on the wrong jobs. Most importantly, this list will stop you from taking the wrong job!

What made that job (or those jobs) so painful for you? The people? The tasks? The commute? The lack of money? Perhaps more important than knowing what you love is knowing what you hate. These are the things that are guaranteed to ruin a perfectly great job for you. We have all been there, but have you ever written down the things you hated? You need to, because a huge part of getting your dream job is making sure you avoid the things you hate. Stop trying to improve in the areas you hate, and stop working on getting better at your weaknesses.

Remember: *you want to do what you love for a living. You do not want another mediocre job. You do not want a knot in your stomach on Monday morning. So make this list and stay true to it. It will save you time during your hunt (keep you focused on jobs that will work for you), and most importantly, make sure you do not end up in another job you hate.*

If you have the time, spend some time on this. A great way to hone in on the things that are guaranteed to ruin a job for you is to look at the job you hated most in your career (**Worksheet 09: The job I hated most as an adult**).

As you work through this section, think about the following examples and determine what matters most to you:

- **Commute:** I will not commute more than _____ minutes
- **Travel:** I will not travel more than _____ %
- **Leadership:** I will not work for another micro-manager
- **Money:** I will not take a salary lower than $_____
- **Personal contribution:** I must work for a company, in a role where I can make a difference
- **Influence:** I must have a voice in my company mission, strategy
- **Career growth:** I must see where I can go with my career
- **Culture:** I will not work in another highly political company
- **Culture:** I will not work in a company where everyone works behind closed doors
- **Culture:** I will not work for another family-owned business
- **Company vision:** I will not work for a company with ever-changing strategic vision
- **Company stability:** I will not work for another start-up company
- **Tools / Resources:** I will not work for a company that does not invest in its technology
- **Tools / Resources:** I will not work for a company that will not invest in tools and resources
- **Training:** I will not work for a company that does not have a training budget

Worksheet 09: The job I hated most as an adult

My Non-Negotiables

Now that you remember what you hate, write it down. What are 10 things you do not want to do? You may be thinking you don't need to write these down, but I see people compromise on their non-negotiables every day, and wake up miserable six months later in the wrong job. Once you have made this list, you need to give it to someone you trust (your champion) and ask them to help you stay accountable to this list.

Worksheet 10: My non-negotiables

Know What You Want

What do you want in your next job? What types of roles and activities do you enjoy doing? Where do you want to go next? Be specific! This list will drive your hunt for a great new job and ensure that you'll take the job that's right for you. Think about what really motivates you. For example, if your last commute sent your blood pressure through the roof, you may say, "I want a commute of less than 30 minutes each way" or, "I want a role where I will be part of the strategic, decision-making process—actively involved in building the vision and mission."

Start with quality of life issues (commute, travel, etc.) and move to the job itself (title, role, tasks, accountability, reporting structure, etc.). Be as specific as possible.

Here are a few things you need to think about:

Company culture

When were you at your best at work? What type of boss inspires you to stretch? What type of culture strangles you and inhibits your productivity and happiness? Company culture needs to be on your list. Often, it is not the job itself that makes people miserable. It's the company's culture (people, processes, what it takes to get things done). Pay attention to those things, and make sure the job activities *and* the environment are a fit for you.

Work/life balance

What does this mean to you? It is different for everyone, and, unless you define it for yourself, how will you know it when you see it? How will you know what questions to ask in the interview process?

Benefits

Benefits may need to be on your list. Do you (or someone who is dependent on you) have a pre-existing medical condition that needs to be covered? You may be limited to which benefits are offered at the company, but you need to understand those options before you take a new job.

Money

Money needs to be on your list, in very specific terms. You need to know the salary you want—and your bottom line (the minimum salary you are willing to accept). Sure, you're learning as you go about what the market will bear and how much you're really worth. Your target salary might shift a bit, but you need to start somewhere. Otherwise, you may either undersell or oversell yourself. You will waste a ton of time interviewing for jobs that will not work for you. Do not wait to talk about salary until a job offer comes along. I will talk much more about this in **"How to talk about money,"** which comes along in **STEP 3: Go Get It**. It will not do you any good to wait until you're offered a job to decide whether or not you'll take it. Negotiating for more money *after* the offer comes in does not work. Many job hunt advice columns say, "Don't talk money! They will lowball you if you do!" That is true, sometimes, for people who do not do their homework. But I am telling you to *do your homework*.

Money matters. Do not sell yourself short. Identify your target, figure out what you are worth, and name your bottom line. Start with your best guess of what you are worth in the market (do Internet research and talk to people). Then, put a stake in the ground that defines how much you want. Next, write down your bottom line. What are you willing to compromise on? It will be an utter waste of your time, and everyone else's if you pursue a job that will not pay you your minimum salary. I see this happen all the time. So, do not spend hours chasing a job that you *hope* will pay you enough.

It's okay if money is high on your list!

Perhaps you are afraid to ask for what you want in terms of salary and compensation. If money is high on your list, that's OK. In fact, I money should be at least number three on your list, unless you have some extenuating circumstances (like Joan, whose story is described below).

There are three issues to consider around compensation:

- What you want
- What you need
- What you're worth

We will explore all of these.

Joan's story:

"I desperately needed a job. I was about to lose my house. My career had never been about money, but I needed it. In reality, money was actually number one on my list, but until I sat down with Catherine and went through this exercise, I had told myself I was open on salary. In reality, I was afraid. I was afraid to limit my job search based on money, and had been spending a lot of time applying and interviewing for jobs I would really enjoy, but should not accept because I would not be able to pay my mortgage. What Catherine helped me realize was that I was pushing myself farther away from my dream job, at the pay I needed and wanted, because I had not claimed those things as my non-negotiable job attributes. When she sat down with me, we looked at my list of what I wanted and how much money I needed. I had written down "open," and had been telling people that. I was getting jobs that were all over the board because I was so open. Catherine pushed me. Finally, I admitted that I actually *needed* a minimum of $80K to pay my bills and save my house. Writing that down and claiming it freed me up to hunt in the right places. Within two weeks, I was interviewing for the job I accepted *and* love one year later."

Figure out what you're worth

To figure out what your target and minimum compensation should be, take these steps:

1. List your past compensation at jobs going back at least five years (you will need this information anyway for most job applications and during interviews). Include starting salary and any raises. Previous paycheck stubs are a good way to figure this out.
2. Write down what you want your compensation to be. What do you feel you are worth? What would make you feel good?

Do a reality check

Determine your market value, as best you can, by doing research. Ask people you know in the industry. Talk to agency recruiters. They are excellent gauges because they have a finger on the pulse of the market.

Identify your bottom line

We all have one. Whether it is $20K or $200K, the important thing is to identify it. If you do not, you will discover how easy it is to take a job for less and wake up wanting more money six months from now. Hopefully, you did a budget when you started this process, so you know what you need to survive, what you need to live, and what you need to save for your future. If you have not done a budget, I highly recommend you stop now and create one.

Write down your target compensation range

If you will be looking at jobs with commission, bonus, or other incentives, write down what that means to you and where you need to be.

Let's take a look at how Joan went through this exercise:

- **Past compensation:**

2001:	$60 - $66K per year
2002:	$66 - 72K per year
2003:	$72K - $80K per year
2004:	$80K per year
2005-2007:	$35K-$45K per year ("I was pursuing an education and my dreams and took a significant hit financially.")

- **What I want:**
  "Emotionally, I thought I was open because there were jobs below $80K that really excited me. However, keeping my house is extremely important to me, so I realize now that I need to find a job that gets me back to a minimum of $80K."

- **What I need:**
  "I need $80K. I have been afraid to put that stake in the ground because I was not sure I was worth it, and I was not sure I could get it. I desperately need a job—no matter what! I thought I needed to go for any possibility. In walking through this exercise, I realize that I have been wasting a whole lot of time applying and interviewing for the wrong positions, taking me away from the jobs that pay what I need. It scared me, but I have put "No less than $80K" as number one on my list of non-negotiables.

- **What I am worth:**
  "Okay. This part is very scary. Am I worth $80K? What if I am not? I really thought the answer would be "No," which is why I have been interviewing for jobs that pay $40-$50K. Well, I did some research. I worked with Catherine to figure out how jobs my skills translate into a position within that salary range. Guess what? I am worth it if I go for a job that combines my previous job at $80K as a project manager and my new education in counseling. Wow! If I just reposition myself, rewrite my resume, and redo my 30-second pitch, I can start going for jobs I will love—at the $80K mark!"

- **My target compensation:**
  $80-$90K

And now you are probably wondering what Joan did with this list.

This is what she did:

"I modified all the worksheets to reflect my new target jobs. I tweaked my 30-second pitch to reflect my new target role. I stopped applying for and interviewing for jobs I would love but could not afford to take. I went back to my network and told them I had done some work and figured out what I really want. Then I shared it with them, and offered some sample job titles and target companies."

"This small change in how I was job hunting made a remarkable difference! Once I repositioned my target list, rewrote my resume to target those jobs and focused my energy toward networking into those jobs, things started happening all over the place. Oh! I really started working my network. Within four weeks, thanks to my network of friends and former colleagues, I was sitting in my dream job! I have been there for 12 months, and I *still* love my job. Plus, I was able to keep my house!"

Okay! Now YOU are ready to commit what you want to paper!

Go do the following worksheet and feel how great it is to claim what you want in your next job.

Worksheet 11: What I want

Now that you have identified what you really want in your next job, you get to write your own perfect job description. This is an important exercise because it will help you hone your search in the right direction and **stop wasting time** looking in the wrong places.

Worksheet 12: My perfect job

Can You Stay Where You Are?

If you are currently working and are not being forced out of a job, staying at your current company is an option.

I ask this question:

Can you stay where you are and get what you want? Should you? Before you jump out into the great unknown, walk with me awhile. Think long and hard about the company where you work. You have invested your heart and soul. You have built relationships. It took hard work and time. Wouldn't it be nice if you didn't have to throw that all away? Be honest with yourself about why you want to leave. What is motivating you? Is it possible to create your dream job there?

People are often surprised to realize they *can* get what they want if they ask for it. If you cannot get what you want at your current company, but your job is stable, you can start talking to people and looking for the right job, safely and confidentially. If your dream job requires further training and/or experience, perhaps you can make that happen while you keep a steady income.

Are there other roles you could play there that give you what you want? Can you ask for more flexibility? Can you share your dreams with your boss and ask for his or her support and guidance in reaching them?

There are two very important reasons you need to think long and hard about this (if you have not already done so):

1. Accepting a counter offer* is almost never a good idea.
2. You do not want to wake up with huge regret about quitting.

*Counter offer: You announce you are resigning and your current boss comes to you with a new, better offer than the one the other company offered you.

The greener grass syndrome

Another problem with not exploring new jobs at your current employer is "buyer's remorse." Call it the rebound job. Call it regret. Call it, "the grass is always greener on the other side." I see it too often to ignore it. Have you been job-hopping? Then you know exactly what I am talking about and you *really* must look at why you've been leaving, what you are searching for, and why you haven't found it. Job-hopping is hurting you and your career in so many ways (of *course* there are exceptions and people with legitimate reasons for apparent job-hopping). But you must ask the questions. Here is what can easily happen to you if you are not very deliberate about this move, and why you are making it:

Tom's story:

Tom jumped into a new job without even considering staying because he was offered an opportunity to move into management and earn more money. He went to a new company expecting, of course, to be very happy. The first few weeks were fine. Then, things started come up. He stayed committed to the new job, but after six months, he felt this way:

- "Wow, nobody seems to care about my ideas here. It is like they don't trust me because I am the new guy."

- "Wow, it is seriously consensus management over here. At my old company, decisions were much easier to get to."

- "I thought I would like working in a new industry, but I don't really like it."

- "I like the short commute and money, but I hate the company culture. People here are really out for themselves."

- "I miss my old company. I had great friends, I knew the channels for getting things done, and people respected my input."

- "My old boss just told me that a new position is opening up in another division and I would have been top on the list. Before I quit, I never even approached him to ask about future career opportunities for me. If I had known they were there, I might have stayed."

Consider the risks

Make sure you are jumping for the right reasons—before you quit. Measure the risk of asking for what you want at your current company. What is the worst that can happen? If you ask for what you want at work (such as a promotion, more flexibility, more money), do you think the answer will be, "no," and you will then get squeezed out? If so, you need to weigh that risk against looking quietly at the outside. Start doing some research and networking. I do not know if it is safe to approach your current employer. In some environments, it is not and you might jeopardize your current job by asking for more. However, at least your decision to ask or not to ask will be a deliberate one and you will not be caught off guard with the counter offer, or with buyer's remorse.

Outside resource

An excellent, quick read on this subject is **The Dip**, by Seth Godin. Godin takes a fabulous look at when to stay and when to quit. If you are restless and unhappy at work and not sure whether you should stay or go, this book might help you make that decision.

In summary, now that you know what you want, if you are still employed, you need to ask yourself, "Can I stay where I am and get what I want?" If the answer is, "Maybe," make a plan to go and get it. Think carefully about how to approach your boss about it, but go get what you want. Understand the risks and be smart about how you go get it.

If the answer is, "No, I cannot stay where I am," the next step is to figure out what you need to do to get your ideal job. The next section will take you through this important exercise.

Do You Want to Start Your Own Company?

Perhaps this chapter has made you realize you do not even want to go get a new job. You want to create your own job by launching a new company, or purchasing an existing one. If this is you, then you are at a very exciting crossroad in your life. Think carefully, make a plan, and be sure this is what you want. The rewards are tremendous, but so are the risks. An excellent book on this topic is *The EMyth Revisited,* by Michael Gerber — a must-read for anyone considering starting or purchasing a company.

Know What You Need to Get the Job You Want

Now that you've done the most important work (identifying what **you** want), you need to see what **employers** want. Just as you want your dream job, employers want their dream employee.

It is powerful to know what you want. Are you feeling good about that? You should be! Hopefully you have some clarity around what you want and what your future holds for you. The next step is to figure out what you need to get that job. In this section, you will explore the required technical skills *and much more*. For instance, your ideal job might be a manager at a small, growing company but your experience has been at larger companies. Small companies typically need leaders who are flexible, creative, and able to wear many hats. Are you able to do that? Perhaps the answer is yes. For example, maybe you launched a new division at an enormous company, playing a role very similar to one at a small company in a start-up division.

Just because you know you've got what it takes to get the job done does not mean that others know that. You need to know what they want, and give it to them.

To get your ideal job you need to:

- Identify the mandatory requirements for the job you desire
- Map those against your current skills, experience and attributes
- Identify any gaps between what you need and what you already have
- Make a plan to overcome those gaps (overcome the perceived or real gaps)
- Know how to translate your value into what employers want

First, identify the skills, experiences and education required for you to get your perfect job. This will help you write a resume that works and say the right things in an interview to get the job. If you don't know what they want, how can you give it to them?

Second, determine whether you have all the qualifications today (most of you will), or whether you need to go get more experience or education to get your dream job. **Worksheet 13: Identify the gaps** will help you do this. Employers are looking for the *best* fit, not just a candidate who *might* fit. Your job is to make sure that you have the right skills, and are able to communicate those clearly and effectively.

Once you know the gaps (or perceived gaps), you'll understand what you must do to overcome the obstacles you may face in your job hunt. All of a sudden, developing your marketing materials (target list, networking plan, resume, and cover letter, among other things) will be quick and easy! You'll learn more in **STEP 2: Know How to Get It**.

Hang in there. All your hard work is going to pay off! These exercises make it easy for you to say, "I'm the one! Look at me! I'll be a superstar for you if you just hire me now!" Once you do these exercises, you will see clearly why you are the perfect candidate.

If you don't understand your gaps or perceived gaps, you may be struggling in your job hunt and not know why. Sadly, if the guy next door is able to express why he is a great fit for the job more clearly than you are, he will very likely get the job offer before you do. Yes, even if he is less-qualified!

Identify the gaps

So, now you are ready to get started. Go to **Worksheet 13: Identify the gaps** and start listing the required skills.

If you need a little help, here is a useful list.

Common gap areas candidates need to bridge:

- **Title:** This is often a language issue: "sales" versus "business development," "Manager" versus "Director." Make sure you speak the employer's language.

- **Industry experience:** Most companies ask for previous industry experience. Sometimes you can overcome this if you are really strong in the other required areas. Again, control what you can control. Maybe the hiring company is light on industry experience internally today and needs to hire someone with years of experience.

- **Compensation:** The more accurately you set your salary requirements, the more success you will have getting interviews. If you ask for $20K more than the market is paying just because you want it, you will likely get cut out of the hiring process. On the other hand, if you ask for $20K less than you are worth, you will likely get less than you are worth. Don't get discouraged. This is what you will be working to avoid with this exercise.

- **Skills:** Are you really lacking the skills required for the job or is there simply a difference in terminology or company jargon? Perhaps, for example, an employer is looking for certain technical skills. If you don't have a particular technology skill, you may have comparable software in your toolkit. Make sure the hiring company knows your comparable skills.

- **Education:** Again, you may have to translate your skills for your audience. Ask if the education requirement is a "nice to have" or a "must have." Sometimes, a hiring manager can hire a candidate who doesn't have the desired education. Other times, it is a mandatory requirement based on human resource and legal constraints. Make sure you know whether it is negotiable or not before you waste your time trying to convince them to look at you despite your lack of a particular degree.

Worksheet 13: Identify the gaps

If there are no gaps between what you want and what you've got, then get going!

If you discover some gaps, **do not give up**! Nothing is insurmountable. If you know what you want, then you **can** go get it! You may need a bridge job or further education to get you there. However, you may not. Understanding these gaps will drive everything in your search, from where you set your expectations to how you present yourself to how you negotiate for what you want. You just need to figure out the gaps and learn how to fill them in.

"How can I find out which skills and experiences I need to have?"

- **Research.** The Internet is an excellent place to do research on which jobs are out there and what they require in terms of experience, skills required.
- **Ask your network.** Ask everyone in your field for their thoughts on what is required for your dream job. Then filter through it and take what makes sense.
- **Test the waters and see what comes back**—in networking meetings, in interviews, when applying for positions. You will learn much as you go. But you need to want the feedback to get it. You have to look for it and ask for it.

"How can I find out if I am underselling or overselling myself?"

- Research
- Ask for feedback, every step of the way
- Keep asking questions and try to read the cues

If, during an interview, you state your salary expectations and the interviewer says, "Great! When can you start?" then you might be underselling yourself.

"How can I pin down the salary range on a specific position?

Keep asking questions once you begin talking about salary. "How do my salary expectations fit with the budget for this position? Am I on the low end or the high end?" "What is the salary band for this position?" "What is the budget for this position?" The person interviewing you may not be willing or able to answer your questions directly (although body language will speak volumes). But if you do not ask, she *certainly* will not tell you. I do not recommend asking these questions during the first interview, but I also would not wait until an offer comes in.

For more information on how to handle compensation issues during the interview process, go to **"How to talk about money"** in **STEP 3: Go Get It**.

"What's wrong with overselling? If I aim high, and I get most of what I want, I'll be happy."

People often ask me, "Why can't I aim high and see what happens?" Well, that depends on how high you are aiming. You *should* stretch, and you can stretch, just not too far. Some people stretch unrealistically and then get discouraged. The problem with stretching unrealistically is that you will not get anywhere near your dream job, because you will get booted out of the hiring process early on. There are a lot of reasons why overselling yourself will stand in your way. The saddest and most detrimental thing about this is that people will rarely tell you why they are booting you out of this process.

"Why won't people just tell me that I am asking for too much money or under qualified for the position?"

You may be wondering "Well, for Pete's sake! Why won't people just tell me that I am asking for too much money, or that I am not qualified?"

Here is a question you need to ask yourself:

"How open am I, really, to feedback?" You might be stopping people from giving you honest feedback because of how you are approaching it. So just make sure you invite the feedback and stay open to it. Then, filter through the feedback and decide what you think is right for you.

Before you blame yourself or get angry with people who give you feedback, let me explain further what stands in the way of getting direct feedback.

Here are some of the reasons you will have a tough time getting this direct feedback:

- **People are nice and they have good intentions**
  Most people who are networking with you or interviewing you are nice people. They don't want to hurt your feelings by telling you that you're not worth what you think you are. So they may not give you the honest feedback you want and need. If you ask for too much money or ask for a role for which you are not yet qualified, interviewers will most likely thank you politely for your time and move on to another

candidate. It is much easier to move on than to tell you that you're asking for way too much. Yes, their desire to protect you is actually hurting you, but realize that their intentions are good. There are very few people who have malicious intent.

- **People do not know the market rates**
  Compensation can be unpredictable. Who talks openly about salary? Unless the interviewer is an agency recruiter finding jobs for a lot of people across the market, the hiring manager may not be confident about the feeling that you are overpricing yourself. She just knows you are overpricing yourself for the job at her company. Some companies pay better than others. Some people just know how to ask for more money. I can tell you this: the same job may pay 10-20% more at one company than another one. Salaries vary from company to company and from person to person.

- **People are hopeful**
  A recruiter or hiring manager may think, "Well, she is under qualified, but maybe I can convince the boss to hire her anyway because I really like her and think she's able to do it."

- **People are often constrained by company policy**
  Most large companies have policies against giving any feedback in the hiring process. Why? Because it's possible to get into big trouble for giving a candidate direct feedback during the interview process. There are laws designed to protect you, the candidate, against discrimination. That's the good news. The bad news is that a company must demonstrate equity in the hiring process. If they give feedback to one person, they need to give it to every candidate. How can a company make sure that each hiring manager is giving back the same type of feedback each and every time? That would be very difficult, especially because each candidate is so different and the feedback would be unique to each candidate (and often subjective).

Hopefully, you now have a better understanding of what you need to do to figure out the gaps (or perceived gaps) in your job search. You will continue to refine your list as you get out there networking and interviewing, but the clearer you are as you set out, the easier this will be.

Overcome the Obstacles

Chances are good that you are missing a few of the skills companies are requiring for your desired job. You now need to think about how to overcome these gaps. Are the gaps real (for example, "A Master's degree is required by all companies for this position, and I do not have a Master's degree.") or simply perceived gaps (for example, "All employers seem to be requiring 3 years of management experience. None of my positions have had "manager" in the title, so I am getting push-back by people saying I am not qualified. However, managing people has actually been a core part of my job for the last 5 years. I just need to find a way to show that in my resume, clearly and concisely, so people will understand that I actually do have the experience).

Here are two examples of people identifying gaps and overcoming objections:

Jane:

Jane was a manager for two years who stepped out of management for a few years. Five years later, she was hunting for a management position because she missed the role and she knew she was a talented manager. The biggest gap Jane faced was fresh, relevant management experience. Employers were concerned about two things:

- "Was she any good as a manager? If she was a good manager, why didn't she stay in the role?"
- "Can she do it? It has been five years. How long will it take her to figure out how to manage people successfully again?" Ultimately, employers wanted to know, "Can we afford to take a risk on her?"

How Jane handled this objection:

"I had a wonderful experience as a manager. I reduced turnover by 15% and increased profitability by 22%. Unfortunately, our industry went into decline and we lost some key customers. The company had to reduce middle management, and I was one of them. I loved the company, so I stayed and moved into another role. When they started hiring for managers again, my personal life was such that I needed to stay in a lower-profile role. I was pregnant with twins and taking care of elderly parents. My personal life is tamer these days, so I have the time and energy to take on that level of responsibility again. I was at my best as a manager and am ready to lead another team to the top. Based on what I am hearing about this position, I know I am well qualified. Would you like some examples of similar challenges I have handled?"

Robert:

Robert wanted to move from the financial industry to the healthcare industry. At first, he was getting a lot of push-back. "You do not have any healthcare experience. We're not interested." Just as he was about to give up, he decided to clearly identify the gaps and figure out how to overcome them. After going through this process, Robert realized that he could overcome the barriers easily. His dream job, IT Director at a healthcare company, required high-volume data transactions, a keen understanding of regulatory issues, and outstanding leadership skills. He could demonstrate experience in all three. All he had to do was translate his background and experience into a language people in the healthcare industry could understand.

How Robert overcame this objection:

First, Robert researched the industry and the companies he was interested in so he could understand the gaps. This entailed online and in-person research with friends and referrals in the healthcare industry. Next, Robert rewrote his resume to reflect what the companies were looking for. The interviews started stacking up and he landed in a job he loves, as an IT Director in the healthcare industry.

Notice that I call these challenges "gaps" and "obstacles," not "brick walls." That is because you will work through them. They will not prevent you from getting a terrific new job. They will just make it a little tougher if you don't address them early on. It is silly to leave them untouched and hope for the best. Once you understand them, you can easily work through the obstacles. This is about awareness and power. You are gaining control of your search.

Remember: *You will get a job. That is not the question. The questions are: "How long will it take?" and "Will it be a job you love?" This 4-step process is all about taking control of your job hunt so that, yes, it will be a job you love and you'll find it faster.*

Next we will talk about your fears. Before you run away, humor me a little. We all have emotional barriers in our lives. Our fear is instinctive and personal. Your fears are unique to you, and they are based upon years of experiences. They are not stupid. They are real. And that is okay. What is not okay is ignoring them and letting them control you and how you find a new job. If you ignore them, they will hurt you. On the other hand, because you are going to read through the next section and decide what to do about them, they will not hinder *you!*

Name Your Fears

You are doing really well with this process! You have already done most of the heavy lifting. There is one thing more we need to talk about before wrapping up **STEP 1: Know What You Want**. We need to talk about your fears. If you do not name your fears and figure out what to do with them, they *will* stand in the way of you getting your next job, let alone your dream job. We all have fear when it comes to big changes in our lives. It is the body's way of protecting us. The problem is, not all fears are well founded. Also, if left unaddressed, they can make your job hunt more difficult than it needs to be.

What are you afraid of? What is the elephant in your sitting room? What is standing in the way of you getting your dream job? What questions do you fear being asked or having to explain in your job search? What is the worst thing you can imagine happening to you as you look for a new job? For some of you, it will be asking for help. For others, it will be meeting new people. For yet others, it will be talking about the fact that you got fired or laid off.

Name your fears. Anticipate hurdles. Own them. Make a plan to overcome them. The reality is that you are going to run into hurdles. However, you can and will overcome them. How quickly and easily you overcome them is up to you. I promise you that every obstacle *can* be overcome. If you name them and practice handling these obstacles before they become an issue, you will move through them quickly. However, if you close your eyes and hope for the best, they will become a real barrier to getting that ideal job. If you get uncomfortable talking about them, so will the person asking you the questions. If you stumble, get too personal or get emotional, then you will raise concerns. Perception is reality most of the time.

Get help! This is where your friends and your champion will be incredibly helpful. Bounce these fears off people you trust and listen to them. Most of your fears are completely unfounded! You just need a fresh perspective to help you see that.

If your fears revolve around interviewing and answering questions about your past jobs, here are some tips. We all have bad things happen in our careers. Do not make a big deal out of it. Do not apologize and the person interviewing you will not make a big deal out of it. On the other hand, if you avoid the question or hem and haw about it, the interviewer will have reason to be suspicious and push you for information until they can get comfortable with it. Perception is reality. If you believe it is a problem, the interviewer will perceive it as a problem.

Tim's story: Two layoffs in three years

> "I have been laid off twice in the last three years. I know that looks bad and I don't know how to explain it to people. I feel like any explanation will make me look like I have something to hide, like I was laid off because I was not a top performer."

The first question Tim needed to ask himself was (because he was thinking it), "Was I performing well? Was I chosen for the layoff because I was easy to replace?" This is a tough question, but one that was brewing underneath the surface anyway for Tim. He was afraid to go there, but if he didn't, it would be haunting him throughout his job search.

As it turned out (even though he was not a top performer), the layoffs had nothing to do with his performance. Both companies made cuts based on tenure with the company, not performance. Once he identified that and looked closely at what he was afraid of, he was able to talk easily with people about why he was laid off.

Also, both layoffs came from small, start-up organizations. While larger firms are no guarantee that there will not be layoffs, he wants to work for a bigger company to feel he has a little more protection from a surprise layoff.

Susan's story: Stay-at-home mom re-entering the workforce

> "I stopped working for seven years to be a stay-at-home mother. I'm ready to get back into the work force. This is what I am afraid of:"

- "People will see me as a flight risk and not want to hire me. I don't know how to convince them I am ready and excited to go back to work."
- "I might not know enough about the industry anymore to be credible in an interview, or on the job."
- "I do not know how to interview well since it's been 10 years!"

How Susan overcame her fears:

- To overcome her fears, Susan practiced talking about her gaps. "My plan was to get my children to first grade and then get back to work. I am very excited that the time has come to go back to work, and I know exactly what I want to do. I loved my job as an accountant and I want to step back into that role where I know I can perform really well, despite having been out of the workforce for seven years. I handle all my family's finances at home, so I have kept up to date with my skills."
- She did research online and informational interviews so she could talk credibly about the industry.
- She read articles and a book on interviewing and practiced until she knew she could handle any questions that came her way.

Greta's story: Perceived job-hopper quitting new job after just three months

"I was miserable at work. I was working wicked long hours and I was not sleeping because I was worried about work. I hated my boss (who was always looking over my shoulder, actually jumping onto my desktop remotely while I was in the middle of work). I hated the company culture, didn't believe in the product they were selling, and felt I was short-changing my clients every day. My commute was 1.25 hours each way. I was angry at myself for taking this job. I had to get out!"

"However, I had some **major fears**:"

- I had only been at this job three months and was afraid I would look like a quitter.
- I was embarrassed that I had even taken this job and I wasn't sure how to explain why I did not ask the right questions during the interview process.
- I had a nine-month gap in my employment just prior to this job that I was afraid to explain. (I left my previous job when my first child was born).
- I felt like a risky hire and was afraid employers would see me that way.

"My biggest fear was getting asked these questions and not knowing how to answer them:"

- "Do you know what you want?"
- "Why did you take a job you hate so much?"
- "Why aren't you giving the job more time?" And the big one, "Are you going to quit if you have another baby?"

I knew I had to quit this job and I did not have time to let these fears stop me from looking, because the longer I waited, the harder it would be.

Greta worked through the "*Change Your Stripes*" process!

- She developed a very clear idea of the job she wanted and wrote it down (she was realistic and specific).

- She wrote down the skills and experience required for that job.

- She identified the potential gaps and made sure she could overcome them with demonstrated career experience.

- She got really honest with herself about why she quit her previous job after the baby was born, why she had taken this job despite her reservations, and why she was quitting now.

- She practiced explaining, clearly and concisely, why she took this job. She had made a very bad choice when she took that job. She had not asked the right questions during the interview process. She hadn't been clear about what she wanted in a job— her strengths and the company culture she needs. Greta landed in what was, for her, a really bad fit. She had learned a painful lesson, and would never make that mistake again. However, it did teach her where she is at her best and what type of role and company she thrives in so that she could sit in front of people, knowing what would be a good job for her.

- She went out to her network, made a list of people with whom she had worked in the past, who knew her and knew how well she delivered. She asked them for help and explained, honestly, what had happened. She asked for their help making connections. They were tremendous! Her network brought her a new job.

Success! Greta started a fantastic new job four weeks later.

You can overcome your greatest fears and go get a job that is right for you – fast. Use **Worksheet 14: Name your fears** to help you take control of these fears and move beyond them.

Worksheet 14: Name your fears

Make Sure You Get What You Want

The Job Hunt Scorecard™

Now that you have a clear sense of what you want, I'd like you to take it and put it into a tool that will help you choose a job that's right for you.

Remember: *This is not just about getting a new job faster. It is also about getting the right job for you. The Job Hunt Scorecard is exactly what you need to help you do that.*

Stay focused on what you want, ask the right questions throughout the hiring process, and make an objective decision about which job will get you jumping out of bed in the morning.

The positive feedback I get over this scorecard is overwhelming. The time you spend creating it is well worth it.

Worksheet 15: The Job Hunt Scorecard™

STEP 2: Know How to Get It

Before everything else, getting ready is the secret to success.

\- Henry Ford

Congratulations on completing **STEP 1: Know What You Want!** I promise, things will be much easier from here. You have done the really tough lifting. Now the fun can begin. Next, you need to know how to go get what you want.

Once again, the work you are doing here will help you work smarter and easier in your job hunt.

Keys to knowing what you want:

Identify your target market

Where are you going to find your perfect job? In this chapter, you will learn how to hunt in the right circles. Pinpoint the people, companies, and groups where you are most likely to find your dream job.

Tell a compelling story

Tell a compelling message about yourself, clearly and concisely, in a way that will resonate with your target market.

Build your communication pieces

- Your 30-second pitch
- Tagline
- Resumes
- Cover letter
- Phone and email introductions

Make a Plan

Make a plan to follow. If you will set daily and weekly goals for activities, you'll know you are taking the right steps toward getting your dream job.

Don't get discouraged

If you have never gone hunting for a job before, then this list can be overwhelming. Do not get discouraged. The exercises in the workbook will help you. No matter what you have done for a living, or where you are in life, you **do** have a compelling story to tell. You may just need a little help telling it. You are unique. You have fabulous talents. In the right job, you will do amazing things for the company that hires you.

Identify Your Target Market

"I don't care how much power, brilliance or energy you have; if you don't harness it and focus it on a specific target, and hold it there, you're never going to accomplish as much as your ability warrants."

— Zig Ziglar, motivational guru

You are well on your way, and ready to identify your target market. Before you can craft your message (tell your story, rewrite your resume), you need to know your audience. That will drive the message you deliver. You want to hit the streets with a message that works.

Building your "target market" means identifying:

- Target job titles or roles
- Target industries & companies
- Target networking contacts
- Target groups and associations

Yes, you will modify your target market as you go along on your job search, but this target market list will get you well on your way and reduce a ton of wasted time and frustration. There are HUGE advantages to having a target market to pursue.

Remember: *This is all about what you want and how to go get it. This is about **loving** what you do for a living, not just getting a job. It really is all about you. If you do not know where you are headed, how will you know where to go? How will you know it when you see it?*

So many people say to me "I'll know it when I see it." Well, **what if you never see your dream job because you are looking in the wrong places?**

The following worksheets will help with your target market:

Worksheet 16: Target job titles or roles

Worksheet 17: Target industries and companies

Worksheet 18: Networking contacts

Worksheet 19: Groups and associations

Explore the following web sites to get some ideas:

Indeed.com – fabulous job search tool that crawls the web searching for open positions.
http://www.indeed.com

CareerBuilder.com - jobs by industry
http://www.careerbuilder.com

Tell a Compelling Story

You are moving into sales mode, ready to work on your self-branding and positioning. In this section, you will capture your personal features and benefits and position yourself to share them with potential employers. Like one zebra trying to stand out in the herd and say, "Pick me!" you need to make sure your unique talents come to life for other people.

In this section, you will put together your marketing materials (your resume and cover letter, among other things) so you can tell a compelling story about yourself. But first, it is time to remember what makes you great. You've got bragging rights! All you need is a little prodding to remember the greatness and write it down. What makes you great? You need to know what makes you great because you are going to sell yourself to a bunch of people who do not know you.

Employers want to know what value you will bring to their organization. Job hunting is all about putting your best foot forward—taking what makes you great and packaging it in a way that resonates with people. Much like selling anything, you need to capture your features and benefits and position them in such a way that other people want to learn more. A simple way to keep your eye on the target while you build your personal brand and marketing message is, "Why should they care?" If what you are saying does not answer that question, you probably need to revise the message.

In this section of the book, I will help you capture what makes you great and turn that into a compelling personal brand.

Know What Makes You Great

Do you know what makes you great? No matter what you have done for a living, there are certainly times when you have gone above and beyond, and really made a difference at work. Start with the fun stuff. The next exercises will help you see and articulate what sets you apart from the masses. Once you know what makes you great and how that pertains to the job you want, you will have a powerful edge over your competition. (Few people do this well, so this is your chance to rise to the top of the candidate pool).

You are unique. Your journey to this stage of your career, no matter how long, is unique to you and nobody else. You need to take some time to reflect on that journey in terms of your accomplishments. This is tough for most people. We work hard, but we do not often stop to capture the accomplishments along the way. They are seen as "just part of the job." Well, now is the time to capture them and brag about them so you can articulate them to people who do not know how great you are. When I interview people, rarely do their accomplishments roll off the tongue. Even when they are clear about what they have accomplished, rarely are they able to explain their accomplishments in clear and concise language, quickly. It takes a bit of practice.

Know Your Proudest Career Accomplishments

Yes, you have some wonderful accomplishments to share! Highlight how your accomplishments stood out against others. Be very specific about *your* contribution, not the *team's* accomplishments. This is not about the team. This is about *your* role on the team and what you did that was above and beyond. People want to hire team players, but when they are hiring, they want to know what will make *you* a valuable member of their team. They also want to understand your level of responsibility. So if your success really was a team success, you need to break down your contribution to that success. The language here needs to be, "I did this." Not, "We did this."

To help jog your memory, here are some typical areas of accomplishment:

- **Going above and beyond.** Did you ever undertake a project that was not part of your responsibility because you liked the challenge? Did you ever make a big sacrifice for your job? What was it and what was the benefit?

- **Identifying problems.** Did you identify any problem that had been overlooked? What was the problem? What was the solution? What were the benefits?

- **Increasing profits.** Did you increase revenue, help generate new revenue stream, rejuvenate a dying product line? If so, how? By how much? (in dollars & percentages).

- **Decreasing spending or saving costs.** Did you save money for the company? What were the circumstances?

- **Increasing productivity.** Did you help increase sales, productivity, and efficiency? How? What were the gains in productivity (in dollars, percentages)?

- **Improving systems or processes.** Did you institute any new systems or changes? Was it your idea? What necessitated the change? Did you lead the system selection and implementation? Who were the stakeholders? What were the benefits to implementing this new system?

- **Preventing big business mistakes**. Did you ever make a NO-GO decision that saved the company money or failure?

- **Training and mentoring:** Did you train or mentor anyone? Were there notable results? Did you develop training techniques? Is your technique being used by others?

- **Suggesting improvements**. Did you suggest any new programs? What were they? What were the results? Did they increase efficiency or sales? Were they published or presented at any industry seminars?

- **Being visionary or strategic.** Did you establish, or help to establish, any new goals or objectives for your company? Did you convince management that they should adopt these goals or objectives? What did it take and what were the results?

- **Getting promoted.** Promotions happen for a reason. Think about your recent promotions and identify what prompted them.

- **Redefining your position or expanding your role.** Did you change the nature or scope of your job? Why or how did you redefine your position? Were there responsibility changes because of this?

If you really struggle to come up with examples, you may need to lean on your champions. Ask people who have worked with you to help you think about your accomplishments. Ask them what they think is great about you. They will likely come up with two or three examples of things you did that were above the crowd.

Top tips for capturing your proudest career accomplishments:

- **Use data (numbers, metrics)** to support your statements and achievements in terms of revenues generated, awards won, and recognition given. If you do not have any data you can reference to support your achievements, simply be as specific as possible. Do not make it up. As you move forward in your career, start grabbing this type of data.

- **Be careful not to share any confidential company data.** Sanitize it. Potential employers will not be impressed if you bring along a former employer's document that is "Proprietary and confidential." They will know you would do the same with their company's confidential documents.

- **Give specific, tangible examples.** It is not enough to say, "I increased sales." You need to say, "I increased sales that year by 23% when all of my colleagues lost 5-25%." Do not just say, "I was number one." Say, "I was number one out of 12 peers."

- **Write down at least three** career achievements. The more recent, the better. However, do not be afraid to share an achievement from a few years ago if it was really noteworthy and pertains to the job you seek.

- **Tailor** these accomplishments to fit your target. Speak in terms your audience will understand.

Worksheet 20: My proudest career accomplishments

Know Your Least Proud Career Moments

Now that you have had a chance to brag about what makes you great, you need to reflect on some not-so-great moments. What are those moments in *your* career you wish you could do over again? We all make mistakes. However, few of us are good at talking about those mistakes. Now is your chance to practice. During the interview process, you will likely be asked to talk about a mistake you have made at work. The more experienced you are, the more likely it is that you'll get asked this question. When people ask this question, they are hoping that you're aware of your mistakes and you learned from them. They want to know that, when you work with them and make a mistake, you will stand up, face it, deal with it, and learn from it (because bad news does not get better with time).

Not only is it okay to have mistakes in our careers, it is necessary! If you are not making mistakes, you are not taking any risks, and you are not moving the business or yourself forward.

There are two reasons to go through this exercise:

- You will be asked, sometime during the hiring process, "Tell me about your least proud career moment" or, "Tell me about the biggest mistake you have made in your career."

It will be a huge relief for you (and very effective) to have some specific examples in your hip pocket. It is tough to come up with an example of a project failure when you are in the middle of a job interview.

- This exercise will likely point to the tasks you do *not* want to be doing. Undoubtedly, your biggest career bloopers involved activities you *do not like*, and therefore, are not very good at. So this is important. Do not be afraid of this question! This is another opportunity for you to solidify what you *do not want* in your next job.

Here is what people are looking for when they ask you this question (and they want to know about a *specific example*, so do not talk in general terms):

- What was the mistake?
- Were you aware of the mistake when you made it?
- Did you acknowledge it at the time or try to hide it?
- Did you try to fix it and did you succeed?
- What did you learn from this and what would you do differently next time?

Bad news: If you get asked this question and are not prepared, you may find yourself saying "I have never made a big mistake. I cannot think of anything. There is nothing I would do differently if I was given the chance." Unfortunately, the person asking the question will be left to wondering whether you pay any attention to the quality of your work and thinking about what you left in your wake. Don't leave them guessing. Tell them how you have handled problems in the past. If you spend some time on this beforehand you will realize that yes, of course you have made some mistakes.

Once again, it is okay if you made a *really big* mistake. When I am interviewing, I expect people to have at least one big bad mistake in their past. Here is why: I need to know that someone is reflective, and interested in learning and preventing mistakes in the future. I also want to know that someone will stand up and admit it when he makes a mistake so we can work together to fix it quickly. Bad news does not get better with time, and when mistakes happen at work, burying them under the carpet is not a good idea. When someone cannot come up with an example like this, it gives me pause and I will dig until I am comfortable with the candidate's ability to recognize and admit mistakes.

Jim's story:

Here is a great answer to the tough question, "Tell me about your biggest career mistake."

The mistake:

"I was at ABC Company as a computer programmer. I was given a project by a Vice President to redesign the small financial tracking system for his division. I knew instantly that I should not do the project without consulting with my manager. However, the VP was a tough customer and I was afraid to tell him that I had to get approval first. So, I went off to my cube, built the functionality he requested, and released it. Of course, when my boss found out, he was very upset that I had not consulted with him. He demanded to know, "Why are you working on a project without consulting with me?" and, "Do you know you just messed up another system in the process?" "Do you also know that this project is a much lower priority than the project I already had you working on?" My boss was made to look bad; I was made to look bad.

"What I did to fix it? I apologized profusely, assured my boss I would not do that again, and asked what I could do to fix it. He told me to take the new release out of operation immediately. I did that, and then I walked into the office of the VP and told him what had happened. I took accountability, told him that I should have stopped and asked the right questions. I told him I would work with the Chief Architect to craft a better solution. Then I went to the Chief Architect to beg forgiveness and ask for help. I asked him for ideas on how we could give the VP what he wanted without jeopardizing other systems. Once we worked out a plan, and a couple of options, I called a meeting with the VP, my boss, and the Chief Architect to walk them through the new options.

What Jim learned from this experience:

"I learned to trust my gut. Follow protocol. If something does not feel right, I need to stop and start asking questions, no matter how upset I make the person who is requesting something of me. It is much easier to handle confrontation when problems are small. It was much harder to sit down with that VP after the fact and tell him that I was taking his system offline."

Now is your chance to prepare for this question. Go to **Worksheet 21: My least proud moment** and see what comes to mind.

Worksheet 21: My least proud career moment

Know Your Strengths

Do you know your strengths? Often the difference between being good and being great is making adjustments that allow you to spend more time developing your greatest strengths.

Did you know that Babe Ruth, the world-famous baseball player, was once a pitcher? At one point he made the deliberate decision to stop pitching so he could focus on batting. He took a lot of heat for his decision because he was a *good* pitcher. He stuck with his decision though, because he knew he had both the motivation and the strength to be a *great* batter.

As you move through this process and into the job hunt, it is helpful to have some of your key strengths on the top of mind. Think about what you have learned about yourself and pick from the list below. If you take a job that will leverage your strengths, you will quickly go from good to great. If, on the other hand, you get a job that requires a number of skills in your weaker camp, you will have a hard time even being good at that job. Beside ability, it is tough to muster the self-motivation to work on your weaknesses. Isn't it far nicer to know that you get to go to work and be great?

Worksheet 22: My personal strengths

Here is a list of common personal strengths to help you pin down your personal strengths:

- Accelerator
- Achiever
- Adaptor
- Advisor
- Analyzer
- Believer
- Budgeter
- Communicator
- Competitor
- Connector
- Consistent
- Counselor
- Creator
- Designer
- Developer
- Doer
- Driver

- Empathizer
- Estimator
- Executer
- Flexor
- Handler
- Idea generator
- Implementer
- Inspirer
- Inventor
- Investigator
- Leader
- Learner
- Listener
- Maximizer
- Mediator
- Mentor
- Motivator

- Navigator
- Organizer
- Persuader
- Persister
- Planner
- Reporter
- Reviewer
- Sensor
- Strategizer
- Team builder

Outside resource:

If you have time and interest in gaining some real insight into your strengths, there are some fabulous resources out there. One of my favorite books is *Strengths Finder 2.0* by Tom Rath. It is a quick read, and comes with a 20-minute online assessment that reveals your top five strengths. The best part is that it also gives you some examples of careers that take advantage of those strengths. It is enlightening to see how accurately this assessment identifies your strengths. Marcus Buckingham also has a great website and several good books on finding your strengths.

Know Your Weaknesses

It is important to get a handle on your weaknesses, because they will haunt you throughout this process if you don't address them. We all have them; they only hurt us when they sit lurking in the corner. Be honest. Be specific. And then practice talking about what you have done to overcome them.

You need to think about your weaknesses for two good reasons:

1   You will get asked about them in interviews, and you want to be prepared for that question.

2   Chances are, your weaknesses stand in your way of happiness and success at work. In fact, your weaknesses are closely aligned with what you hate doing.

Doing this exercise will help you stay clear on what you are not good at, and hopefully, avoid those things in your next job. For example, if you are a "visionary," you are probably not good at the detail work. Taking a job that requires you to do a huge amount of documentation would not be a good fit for you.

Know Your Features and Benefits

Do you know your own features and benefits? The next few sections are designed to capture them so you can package yourself well when you are ready to write your resume, cover letter, and other communication tools. Too often, people jump right in to writing their resumes and miss some key experiences, training, and awards.

Awards and Recognition

It is time for you to boast. Write down any recent awards and accomplishments. Put them all down on paper. Some of them may be keys to helping you get the position you desire. Some will not be of value and don't need to be on your resume. For example, perhaps you got an award for something you actually hated doing. You won't want to advertise that award. For now, and for your own reference, it is a best practice to capture all of them because you never know when one of these awards will pertain to your career later on.

Please note: If you haven't received any rewards or recognition, do not despair! Not every company is good about recognizing great people. That may be why you're looking for something new. Plus, you are about to start collecting awards and recognition because you are about to land your dream job (and that is what going for great in your job hunt is all about). If you are in your dream job, you will excel and achieve great heights in your career.

Training

Put it all down and use that master list as a reference to tweak your resume as needed for various positions.

Notable skills

I recommend that you list every skill you possess based on your recent work history (last five to ten years). You will whittle it down to the most important ones when you write your resume, but you may have an obscure skill that sets you apart from the rest and gets you the first interview. For example, you might have experience selecting a charity for your company. It may be entirely out of scope for your dream job, but a nice sideline project you led. Perhaps your ideal company is in the process of selecting a charity. If you have it written down on your list, you will be able to reference it quickly.

Make note, especially, of these skills:

- Soft skills (leadership, planning, execution, team-building, dependability, etc.)
- Technical skills (know what matters to your industry and the role you are pursuing)
- Industry experience

Worksheet 24: My features and benefits

Tell Me About Yourself ... in 30 Seconds or Less

Defining what you want is the most important thing in your search for a new job. Developing a 30-second pitch is the **second most important thing**. Yes, it is more important than your resume. It should be fairly easy now that you've done some of the hardest work. Your 30-second pitch is what you tell people when you meet them and they ask, "What are you looking for?" or, "Tell me about yourself."

Start by answering this question:

"If I can remember only one thing about you when I walk away today, what would you like it to be?"

Think of this as your 30-second commercial. You are the product. This is the label or ad you put out there to attract potential buyers. Short, sweet, and to the point. This will be the first thing people hear about you, and the thing they will remember most about you, which is great if you have a good one. Ideally, you want a little tag line that is memorable. Mine is, "I'm a Stripe Changer. I help people get their dream job."

Your 30-second pitch needs to be clear, concise, and easy to understand. For example, if your mother cannot understand what you want for a job, you need to rewrite your pitch until she does. Keep it simple, and make sure people who are not in your field understand it. Why? Because the people outside of your industry or area of expertise will very often put you in touch with the right people. You may find this hard to believe, but it is true.

Look once again at your target. **What do you want?**

Sample template for your 30-second pitch:

- "Hi, my name is _____."
- "I am a _____(something catchy and memorable if you can – a tagline)_____."
- "I am on the hunt for ___(job title works well here)_____."
- "I am looking for networking contacts like ____(tell people how they can help you get what you want)_____."
- "In short, I bring _____(a *very high-level view* of your background)____."
- "For fun, I _____(something unique about me is)_____."
- "How can I help you?"

Create a tagline

This is going to be tough to do, and you can certainly come back to this later. However, it is ideal for you to have something memorable to say, in one sentence, that captures who you are. For instance, a financial planner who works with young people might say, "I am a dream builder." In contrast, a financial planner who works with small business owners or retirees might say, "I am a wealth protector." A computer support company might say, "We work hard so you don't have to." Think about your target market. What is one thing that they care about? What is one thing that will capture their attention?

Here are some examples:

Jane, a realtor

> "Hi. My name is Jane Doe. I am a dream catcher. I help first-time home buyers get their dream house without breaking their piggy bank. I've been in this market for 15 years and love guiding people to the right neighborhoods for their personal lifestyle. I would appreciate any referrals to first-time home buyers or mortgage brokers.

Sam, a used car salesman
> "Hi. My name is Sam Doe. I help cars find their second home. I love what I do, but I don't love my company. I would appreciate any referrals to a used car dealership you enjoyed working with."

Bob, a computer security expert

> "Hi. My name is Bob. I stop computers from giving away your shoe size and net worth. What I am looking for is a new job in IT security at a small or medium-sized company. I would appreciate any referrals you can offer me in technology. Anyone you know in IT will do because I am sure they will be able to direct me to the right person in their company."

Too cute for you? That's fine. Say what makes you comfortable. Then, push the envelope a little further. Make a fun one and try it out. See what happens. At least you now have an idea and you can see how people will remember Jane, Sam and Bob better than their competitors. A little humor in your job hunt is a good thing. People like to laugh, and if you can make them laugh in an easy and professional manner, they will appreciate it and remember you—and help you!

Okay, so it is time for you to tell the world, in 30 seconds or less, what make you great. Of course this will be a work in progress and you will tailor your 30-second pitch as you meet with different audiences. However, if you give yourself something to start with, your job will be much easier when you hit the streets to go find a great new job.

Worksheet 25: My 30-second pitch

Write a Target Marketing Plan

You are now ready to tell the world what makes you great! A target marketing plan can help you do this. It will help you take your talents and newfound confidence to the streets.

I love reading people's target marketing plans. Because I am passionate about helping people expand their networks, this document (in conjunction with a resume) helps me to help you. Sure, I can look at your resume and make some assumptions. But if you spoon feed me your target market and desired roles, I immediately think of companies and people you should connect with. This will help to keep you, and your network, focused. It is amazing how the networking takes off once you start sending one of these around.

To create your marketing plan, use your target list and the worksheets on what makes you great. Use the template in **Worksheet 26: My marketing plan** to help you build your own target market list.

Once you have completed your target marketing plan, share it with your network. Review it with them and get their ideas and opinions. Your list will undoubtedly expand as you go—in the *right* directions. No more wild goose chases because you know what you're after and where to go get it. Once you start to share this plan, so will the people who want to help you.

Here is an example:

John Doe – waiter – fine dining

123 Juniper Lane
Minneapolis, MN 11111
johndoewaiter@johndoe.com
Cell: 123-123-1234

Hello! I am looking to make a career move, and am reaching out to my network to find potential opportunities. I would really appreciate any assistance you can provide. I have summarized my networking goals, as well as my skills and accomplishments. Please feel free to share this with anyone you think might be interested in connecting with me.

In short, I am a top-producing waiter with a loyal customer base and a passion for creating memorable dining experiences. I am looking for a position at an upscale restaurant in the metro area. I am studying to be a wine steward and plan to open my own restaurant by the age of 40.

Target positions / roles / job titles
- Lead Waiter

Samples of target companies
- The little table restaurant
- Fine dining incorporated
- French garden
- Delicate dining

I would like to meet these networking contacts
- Restaurant owners
- Managers and waiters at fine restaurants
- People who eat at fine restaurants and can recommend their favorites
- Wine distributors
- Food distributors

Sample career accomplishments
- Designed loyalty program at Dining Delight, increasing revenues by 22%
- Increased profit margin on wine sales 7% by streamlining the wine list and negotiating with vendors

Thank you very much for your time and consideration. I appreciate any support or suggestions you can send my way! I hope to see you soon at a table near you.

Kind regards,

John Doe

Worksheet 26: My marketing plan

Stop. Take a break.

Don't you feel wonderful? You should. If you don't, go walk through those career accomplishments again. Better yet, go call your champion and talk about what you've been up to. Tell someone what you've just learned about your target market and yourself. And then stop. Take a break. And go do something nice for yourself.

Write a Resume that Works

Are you ready? It's time to capture your background and expertise **as it relates to what you want** and **as it demonstrates your value-add** in the form of a resume. What's "value-add"? It is what makes you unique, what makes you a particularly valuable employee. For some, it is your vision. For others, it is your ability to build and motivate teams. For yet others, it is your dependability, how you show up and deliver as promised. People don't want to know that you're just like all the rest of the candidates out there. They want to know what makes you different and worth noticing. Once again, you must translate your skills and expertise into terms your audience can understand. They are tough to write. The great news is that the work you've done so far will help you write a powerful resume that differentiates you from your competition.

Before we begin, let's start with some pretty basic, but important questions:

"What is a resume?"

A resume is really only three things:

- A tool to get you an interview, not to get you hired

- About where you want to go, not where you have been

- A chance to share a *snapshot* of what you accomplished for your former employers … not about your job descriptions.

A resume is not …

- A complete history of your career from beginning to today

Why? The main reason your resume should just be a snapshot of your background and experience is this:

YOUR RESUME WILL GET ONLY 5-15 SECONDS of a recruiter or hiring manager's review the first time they look at it. Then, you will either go into the "call now" pile, the "maybe later" pile or the "not for this job" pile.

"Why is a resume important?"

A resume is important because, like a business card, a resume is an expected part of the interviewing and hiring process. It is your tool to get in front of people, compel them to want to learn more about you and to give them a reason to believe you are the best candidate for the job.

"How and when should you use a resume?"

You should use a resume in the following three scenarios:

- To network: your resume is a tool to let people know the skills and expertise you have, so they can help you find new connections in the same space.

- To give to recruiters and employers: you will give your resume to recruiters and hiring managers to get interviews and referrals.

- To apply for jobs: a resume is an expected part of every application process

Now that we have clarified what a resume is, and how to use it, let's get into what you really want to know … how to write a resume that will get you the interviews you want.

I believe there is a 4 step process to writing an effective resume:

1. Know what you want

2. Know what employers want

3. Know what makes you great

4. Create your resume – and tell them why you are a great fit for the job

Guess what. You have already done steps one through three! You are ready to start writing your resume! Use these worksheets as your guide:

Worksheet 13: Identify the gaps

Worksheet 16: Target job titles or roles

Worksheet 17: Target industries and companies

Worksheet 20: My proudest career accomplishments

Worksheet 24: My features and benefits

I highly recommend that you go do some research, find 5-10 jobs that you like, and redo **Worksheet 13: Identify the gaps**. It is highly likely that you now have a better sense of what job you want, and will modify this worksheet. So do that now.

And now, you can use **Worksheet 27: My resume** to start putting the pieces together, in the correct order.

Now, with these worksheets as your guide, follow these simple steps to create a winning resume every time:

1. Find a resume template you like (I prefer one that is a blend between functional and chronological resume)

    a. Do an advanced search on Google for someone with skills like yours: File type document, "market research analyst"

    b. If you use Microsoft Word, there are a bunch of good resume templates out there.

    c. OR you can google "resume template" and get some great templates

2. Write your name, contact information (the trend these days is to avoid putting your mailing address on your resume, especially if you are posting it online. Cut down on identity theft and hold this personal information until you are engaged in an interviewing process with a company).

3. Write a professional summary – geared toward the job you want!

4. Showcase your career highlights:

    a. Take your proudest career accomplishments – and put them here.

5. Key skills

    a. List your top 10 skills … the ones employers want you to have, IN THEIR LANGUAGE

    b. This is the keyword game

6. Work history

    a. Be Brief!

b. List Job title (industry-generic)

c. Share dates (most advisors say years only, not months)

d. List employer name

e. Location of job (city, state) optional

f. BRIEF description of your role – unless it is the obvious!

g. Use bullet points when you can

h. Highlight brief examples of your successes. Share very briefly, and with specific examples, what you did that was above and beyond, or unusual, or simply a job well done … as it pertains to the job you want NOT the one you had.

i. Use any data you can to support your claims (increased revenues, increased productivity, or recognition. Do whatever you can to demonstrate the value you added to the company).

7. Training – if employers want to see training, or if you feel it is important

8. Education

9. Do not list references on your resume! Simply state "available upon request."

Look at other people's resumes in your industry to get ideas on how to represent yourself well. There are a few sample resumes here, but your background and experience are unique. Lean on friends who have similar backgrounds and do some research on the Internet to find resumes that work well for you.

Small, but noteworthy suggestions on what to call your resume when you save it:

Keep your resume name simple and easy to recognize, at a glance. It is *your* resume. Personalize it. For example, "JohnDoe" or "JaneDoeMarketingPro" or "JimmyDoeITProjectManager" or "JanieDoeSales052008."

These suggestions all include your name, clearly stated and easy to find. When I get a resume that is saved as "myresumev9" or "Finished Resume," it slows me down. A file like this might go in my "deal with this later" pile, because I need to resave it with your name on it so that I can find it later. You do not want your resume to end up in the "deal with it later" pile. Worst-case scenario, I will not be able to find your resume when I do have your dream job. My success is dependent upon my ability to find you later, so I usually rename it and create a contact for you, but not always. And, I can assure you that hiring managers and people in your network are not working so hard to make your resume accessible.

Keep it professional. "Super Suze Problem Solver" is cute for a tagline when you are meeting people in person, but not for a resume.

Top ten resume tips

1. Design your resume to get you an interview, not to get you the job. A good resume should offer a quick snapshot of your background, not an itemized account of everything you did for the last 10 years. Give just enough information to pique interest. Make potential employers want to call you to learn more.

2. Keep it simple and clean, with a lot of white space. You can find free templates in your word processing software, on the Internet (simply search on "resume template" for some excellent choices), or from a friend. Make sure your resume is clean and easy to read.

3. Focus on your accomplishments, not your job description. What did you do for the company to drive revenue, increase productivity, or reduce waste? What were the benefits to your previous employers with you on board? Use key words; not full sentences. Refer to the workbook exercises you have already done for key words. Use bullet points, columns, and lists instead of long sentences.

4. Use words sparingly. Make sure you are not duplicating your skills. If you did the same activity in several jobs, condense and put at the top in a "key skills" section, or simply list in your most recent job.

5. Do not use generic job descriptions. Do not tell your audience the obvious. For example, it is pointless for a sales person to list "managed customer relationships." (If a sales person is not doing this, she is failing!). The right audience knows what your title means. Include something they do not know about your role. For example, a sales person should mention size and type of client, the size of his "book of business," close ratios, etc.

6. Open with a brief professional summary (your tagline and 30-second pitch will help you come up with a compelling summary) and follow with a hit list of your career accomplishments. What makes you great?

7. Consider a functional resume format, with skills and accomplishments at the top and a very brief chronology beneath that, listing where and when you worked. This is my favorite style. Capture what you bring to the table as it pertains to what you want. (See the sample below.)

8. Get someone to edit your resume! Make sure you don't have any typos ("Spell check" cannot be trusted to catch all spelling or grammatical errors). Do not use company-specific lingo or acronyms (like SFP for sales force process).

9. Always be honest. Not only is it the right thing to do, it will come back to haunt you if you lie or misrepresent your experience on your resume.

10. Do not show your references on your resume. Protect them by not sharing them until you are having serious hiring conversation with a company.

Professional Summary

If you are a seasoned professional, it is a good idea to have a brief professional summary at the top of your resume. Basically, take your dream job key skills required and brag about yours in your professional (executive) summary. Here are some sample summaries.

Sales person: Top sales producer. Increased sales by 23% in a declining industry. Reduced administrative costs by developing process improvements. I help companies grow their bottom line.

Marketing Leader: I seize market opportunities. As a leader, I empower my team members to see and capture new revenue opportunities before the competition does. One of my market communications managers came to me with a new product opportunity in 2006. Together, we crafted a project profile, gained sponsorship and budget, and developed a new product line that generated $1.3M in its first year.

Business Leader: I fix business problems. Gifted at seeing a potential roadblock before it surfaces, and then shaping and driving the solution. In recent years, that gift has enabled me to drive the turnaround of a product line from a 23% decrease in revenue to a 47% increase in revenue over the last two years.

Sales and Marketing Director: Accomplished strategic marketing professional known for growing market share around the world. Extensive consumer packaged goods experience. Classical and alternative marketing training and expertise. Over six years of full Profit and Loss responsibility at the division and major product line levels. Highly skilled in areas of leading new product ideation, product positioning, pricing, promotion, customer segmentation, retention/up-sell, brand design & essence and advertising & sales tool communication strategy.

Sample functional resume

Here is an example of a well-written functional resume.

Jane Doe - Seasoned marketing professional

Summary

Sales & Marketing professional with proven ability to see, and seize, market opportunities. From strategic planning to inspiring individual contributors to creating and delivering innovative product solutions, I remove barriers and provide vehicles for success. I also excel at strategic partnership development and brand innovation. I am known as a confident change agent and innovator who is capable of achieving results in both structured and unstructured situations.

Functional expertise:

- Marketing strategy, planning, and execution
- Channel marketing
- Vendor selection and management
- Collateral development

- Market research
- Creative planning and execution
- Budget development and management

Industry experience

- Retail
- Healthcare
- Public Relations
- Finance

Career Highlights

As marketing lead over new initiative to rejuvenate declining brands, increased market share by 32%
- As project manager responsible for identifying emerging markets, drove the planning, development and execution—resulting in the development and launch of three new product lines. First year sales on these products lines totaled $1.3M

Work Experience

2006-present Senior Manager, Market Research.
ABC Company, A leading innovator in retail electronics

As senior manager, I look for new product opportunities, as well as market penetration opportunities. I created a new Market Opportunity Group and merged three other groups together. These changes resulted in increased productivity and cost reduction.

Responsibilities include:

- **Strategic vision:** fundamentally involved in upper management discussions and setting corporate strategy

- **Efficiency, cost savings and productivity gains:** reduced cost of quantitative studies by 60% and enforced 10-day standard turnaround; stretched $1M budget into 64 primary research projects

- **Communication:** Bridge the gap between market need and business capability, from engineering and product managers to CEO

2001-2006 Marketing Manager
Front and Center incorporated, an IT services firm

As the head of marketing for this IT services firm, I led a team of seven employees to:

- Contribute to a 70% annual revenue growth.
- Conceive marketing strategies and implement tactical plans that support business goals and objectives.
- Define key performance indicators to measure sales and marketing results and operations.

- Build and manage an inside sales team.
- Create processes and materials for lead generation and qualification.
- Select and implement sales force automation system, resulting in reduced length in sales cycle.
- Initiate and leverage relationships with key industry media and analysts.
- Spearhead corporate events including customer conferences, trade shows, and webinars.
- Manage internal and external marketing initiatives, including graphic design, web development, public relations, and advertising resources.

1994-2001 Senior Market Planning Consultant
ABCD healthcare firm

- Developed marketing plans for major corporate initiatives. Plans included market analysis, growth objectives, cost benefit analysis as well as pricing, product and promotional strategies.
- Provided comprehensive marketing counsel and project management.
- Analyzed market opportunities; developed and managed new product/program market introductions.
- Led cross-company teams focused on successful implementation of marketing plans. Drove changes in existing business processes where necessary.
- Specialized in affiliate company marketing. Directed interrelated marketing efforts involving company affiliates, subsidiaries or partners.

"How do I make sure I am reaching my audience?"

- **Research.** The Internet is your friend here. Search for 5-10 jobs that interest you. Take a look at the job requirements and put those down on this list. Search online for resumes (you will be shocked at what you find) and see what others in your field are doing. Do not copy! Just note some good ideas.

- **Ask people.** Your network is your friend. Ask for feedback on your resume—every step of the way!

- **Make several versions.** Yes, I'm serious. If you're smart, you'll have several different versions of your resume based upon various jobs you're going for. The brutal reality is that you need to play the keyword game. Your resume must be easy to read and compelling. If not, it will go to the "maybe later" pile, never to resurface again. Also, be sure your resume is in these three formats:
    o .pdf (if you have it)
    o Microsoft Word®
    o Text

- **Before you submit a resume for a specific job, make sure you have the skills listed, as they are required.** If, for example, they want 10 years of sales experience, having "10 years of business development experience" will not work. Only "10 years of sales experience" will work. Your resume needs to show that you have 10 years of sales experience. If your resume does not have "sales" in it, you may not even get in front of the recruiter (if you apply online, you will get sorted out of the system. Online application systems sort by keyword relevance. Even if you get in front of a recruiter or hiring manager, they might put you on the "read later" pile.

You do not want to be on the "maybe later" pile. Recruiters, and especially hiring managers, rarely get to those piles, because the pile of "these look great" resumes get the interviews and recruiters stop looking.

Get Business Cards

I often get asked "do I really need business cards?" The answer is "Yes!" You need business cards. No matter what you do for a living, you need a business card to leave behind so people remember you and know how to find you. I love to see contact details on the front, with a tagline and three notable things about you on the back. What are three things you want people to remember about you? Those are good bits of information to put on the back.

Where to get business cards:

- Your local office supply or printing store.
- Online. You will likely find the best deal online, but they will take time to get.
- Make your own. You can buy business card kits at office supply stores.

Make a Plan

"If you do not design your own life plan, chances are good that you will fall into someone else's plan. And guess what they have planned for you? Not much."

-Jim Rohn

You are ready to go get that job you want! You've done a lot of work, so pat yourself on the back. You have actually done the hardest and most important work. That is terrific! Now, let's channel that energy into a job hunt action plan to get you there. As you know, The *"Change Your Stripes"* process is all about being smart with your time. Once you dip your toe in, you will quickly get distracted by *well-intentioned people* and *potential opportunities*. Keep your head in the game and stay on track by building a **Job Hunt Action Plan**. Don't wait for the perfect plan to come together. Some of you are going to get stuck in "analysis paralysis." There is no such thing as a perfect plan. You are aiming for good, not perfect.

"A good plan today is better than a perfect plan tomorrow."

- George S. Patton

Your commitments to yourself

Before we flesh out your job hunt plan, let's talk about personal commitments. You have come this far because you care about the next job you take. You care about the life you live. So, commit to what you will accomplish each day and each week. You know your danger areas. Own them. Make a commitment to yourself to overcome those areas so you can get a job you'll love. Fast. Yes, this is about you. Right now. If you are unemployed, you need to make some big commitments (unless you have a huge financial cushion and do not need or want a job anytime soon). If you are gainfully employed and you don't believe you are in danger of losing your job, your time commitments can be smaller. You can focus on expanding your network and hunting for that next great job.

Time commitment: If you are unemployed and need a job soon, you must work 40 hours a week on your job hunt. No excuses. No laundry or playing during the day. Job-hunting is your full-time job right now. You need to treat it that way. Set those expectations with other people in your life as well. Let your family and friends know that you have made a commitment to yourself to job-hunt 40 hours a week and, no, you are not available to run errands for them (extenuating circumstances aside). You need to set boundaries for yourself and others.

Worksheet 28: My commitments to myself

Your Job Hunt Action Plan

Like all good things in life, smart job hunting takes a little planning. If you head out on vacation without a plan or a roadmap, then you will very likely end up in the wrong place, off the tracks, and you'll get to your destination the hard way. Job hunting is no different.

As you make this plan, tailor it to *you*. Acknowledge your strengths and weaknesses. If you are great at meeting people, crank up the number of face-to-face meetings and networking groups you'll attend. If you hate meeting people, crank up the online social networking. Figure out how to ask your network for help and maximize those relationships. If you are a strong writer, spend more time crafting memorable follow up notes and perhaps publishing an article or two in your industry.

Sample Job Hunt Action Plan

How I will spend my time:

Networking   80%

Internet research   20%

Week One:

- Ask _____ to review my resume
- Ask _____ to review my marketing summary
- Create and order business cards
- Start reaching out to my network and setting face-to-face appointments
- Selectively post my resume online (More details in the "Online" section)
- Set up job agents online

Daily goals:

- Twenty phone calls per day
- Five personal connections per day (over the phone or email; phone is ideal)
- One in-person meeting (networking or interviews) per day

Daily schedule:

From	To	Action
7:00 AM	8:00 AM	Breakfast
8:00 AM	9:00 AM	Check and send emails
9:00 AM	11:00 AM	Make networking calls
11:00 AM	12:00 PM	Make notes, send follow-up emails
12:00 AM	1:00 PM	Play, relax, or have networking lunch
1:00 PM	4:00 PM	Meet, network, interview
4:00 PM	4:30 PM	Send thank-you notes, email, & return phone calls
4:30 PM	5:00 PM	Make "to-do" list for tomorrow

Note: You are not allowed to beat yourself up during this process. If looking at this sample action plan makes you short of breath, push some items into week two. Set yourself up for success, but push yourself as well.

Worksheet 29: My job hunt action plan

It takes as much energy to wish as it does to plan.

- Eleanor Roosevelt

STEP 3: Go Get It!

Nothing in the world can take the place of persistence. Talent will not; nothing is more common than unsuccessful men with talent. Genius will not; unrewarded genius is almost a proverb. Education will not; the world is full of educated derelicts. Persistence and determination alone are omnipotent.

- Calvin Coolidge

Are you excited? You should be! You have worked very hard (yet smart!) thus far. Now is the fun part. Now you actually get to go after that job you want, tell people about it, and see the magic start to happen. Of course there will be good days and bad, but you are clear on what you want. Now is the time to go get it.

Top tips to remember while you are on your hunt

- **Persistence pays.** What Calvin Coolidge says about life pertains to the job hunt tenfold. Remember that every time you get discouraged. Do not give up. Your dream job is waiting just around the corner. So keep walking!

- **Job hunting is really just people meeting people!** The thing to remember about hunting for a new job is that all the people you meet are people too, with happy and sad places of their own. Meet people on their level, as yourself, and you will connect with them. Relax and enjoy getting to know new people to see if you want to work with them. Want to know a little secret? Many of the people you meet will be just as nervous as you are about making a great first impression. **Even some of the people *interviewing* you will be nervous about meeting you!**

- **You can have power** in your job hunt! People ask me all the time, "Why do employers have all the power in the job hunt process?" The answer: Because you give it to them! If you know what you want and how to clearly communicate it, then you are in control of most of your job hunt. The more you prepare for the hunt, prepare for each meeting, and ask the right questions, the more power you have. This process is a two-way street.

- **Take great care of your network.** Keep track of who you talk to, how they helped you and how you can help them.

- **Manage your reputation**. It is up to you to take care of your reputation. This means being judicious with your online and offline presence. It means being professional everywhere you go and treating others as you would have them treat you. It means making promises you can keep. When you tell a close friend you're looking for a new job, he will probably forward your email to other people and may not think twice about sending it as it is, with an off-color joke or whatever casual thing you sent to your friend. That email can make its way to an HR manager or potential manager at your dream company and you will not be looked upon favorably. So, think before you speak or hit "send." If you maintain a personal web site, or participate in any of the online social networking groups, make sure you and your friends are presented professionally. Like it or not, you are judged by the company you keep, both on and off the job.

Now, I will walk you through your job hunt. I'll tell you which steps to take first, and be there to guide you through each and every one of them. I'll enlighten you ("What on earth is going on inside that company? I had an interview two weeks ago and have not heard back!") I'll answer questions, and give you tips on how to make the most out of every stage. In this chapter, I'll help you spread the word, find the jobs, network, apply with panache, interview for success, and lastly, choose the job that's right for you.

Go Yell it From the Mountain!

You are now ready to go find that job. You're on your way! The time has come to tell everyone what you're looking for and what you've got to offer. You've got your act together. You know what you want, you've got a great story to tell and all you need to do is get in front of people. It is time to go make things happen.

If you do not tell everyone you know, everyone you meet, that you are looking for a new job, you just might miss out on your next great job! You have a 70-80% chance of finding your next job through someone you know—but only if you tell them.

I wrote this as a stand-alone section because I think it is important. Many people are shy about the fact that they are looking for a new job, whether they are unemployed or looking while still gainfully employed. Don't be shy or apologize. Be excited, and tell people you are excited. Because you are no longer in a position of "I need a new job." You now know what you want, clearly and concisely. Hopefully, you can taste what life will be like on the other side, once you have landed that dream job. This is exciting, and you should share that excitement with people so they can help you find and land your dream job.

If you do not tell everyone you know, and everyone you meet, that you are looking for a new job, you might miss your perfect job!

84% of people are still searching for their dream job according to a recent survey by careerbuilder.com. That means, in short, you are not alone! There is absolutely no shame in announcing that you are looking for something new. In fact, most people will be eager to help you because they either need help right now in their own job hunt or they expect to need help in the future. Most of the people you meet have been in your shoes at some stage of their career.

In summary, especially if you are unemployed, you must tell everyone you meet that you are on the hunt for something new. There is no shame in looking for your dream job, let alone a new job. Gone are the days when you can expect to stay with one company for 30 years. It just is not going to happen. Most of us will be unemployed at some stage of our lives. It is the new world order.

Go Find the Jobs

Remember: You want to work smart, not hard, in your job search. Looking in the right places is a huge part of that. So, where do you go look to find the jobs you want? First, do not start online. Please, do not start online. You will quickly get lost, and drawn away from your target. Let's take a peek at where you should go hunting, in order of importance.

First, let me share some statistics with you. There are many studies out there on where people find jobs. The statistics vary, although only slightly.

I have taken an average from several reputable sources, and here are the numbers:

- 70-80%   Networking
- 45-50%   Targeting companies directly
- 5-15%   Answering ads in local newspaper
- 5-15%   Recruiters (Search firms and agencies)
- 5-20%   Internet
- 5-10%   Answering ads in a trade journal

Where do you want to spend your time? Pick four methods you are going to use consistently. Write them down. Let's take a peek at where you should go hunting, in order of importance.

Remember: We are focused on working smart, not hard. Looking in the right places is a huge part of that.

- **Networking**
  Spend 80% of your time networking, and you will find your dream job faster.
- **Groups and associations**
  Local organizations, trade groups, user groups, networking groups, and job transition groups make up a powerful network of people for you. With a little research and some deliberate outreach, you can get connected to the right people and keep your network expanding in the right direction.
- **Company web sites**
  Company web sites are an important part of your job hunt, if you focus on your top 5 or so target companies.
- **Online (research and job boards)**
  Depending on how you approach it, the Internet can either be your friend or your enemy during your job hunt.
- **Trade and business publications**
  It is a good idea to be well read in your industry, especially while you are on the hunt for something new. It will help you connect, help you prepare for interviews, and help you be picky about *where* you interview.
- **Recruiters**
  You will deal with recruiters at every stage of your job search. Both external and internal recruiters can be a wealth of information, and an advocate for you. Pay close attention to the upcoming section on working with recruiters to make sure you maximize every connection with recruiters.
- **Job Fairs**
  Job fairs are coming back in style. They offer a great opportunity to network, practice your 30-second pitch, and explore potential company connections. They are also highly competitive, so be sure to dress for success and go prepared. I recommend you review the company list ahead of time and make a plan of attack by identifying your goal in attending, as well as which companies you want to target. Employers will be impressed to hear that they are on your short list.

Network for Success

Networking is simply the most effective way to find a job. Spend 80% of your time networking, and you will find a new job much faster and easier. In a recent survey I conducted, I asked people who landed new jobs "What are the most valuable lessons you learned in this job hunt?" Overwhelmingly, the answers were around networking.

Here are the top recommendations:

- Do not wait to start networking. Attack it aggressively.
- Find out about the network groups and how you can get invited quickly (some groups are "invitation only;" some only happen every two to three months).
- Network with people who are employed, not just others who are in transition. People who are working are important for your networking activities.
- Stay connected with positive people who want the best for you, the individual (your champions!).

The term "networking" is overwhelming to most. It does not have to be. In this section, you'll learn how to get started networking, and how to maximize those connections. The key is to start with people who know you and believe in you—then ask for their help. You will discover that people are excited to help you, and will do more for you than you ever imagined. All you have to do is ask. Most people need a direct request. Arm the people in your network with a clear and concise message they can take to the streets on your behalf.

Why is networking so effective? Three reasons:

- **People who know you will go out of their way to help you find a great new job.** They believe in you. They understand your strengths and will get you to the decision maker more often than you can, cold off the street.

- **When you are personally referred to a hiring manager, you will move to the top of the candidate pile.** It will not guarantee you the job, but it will almost always get you serious consideration.

- **Companies will hire a referred candidate over an unknown candidate when they can.** Why? It reduces their risk. If someone who knows their company and culture recommends someone, the chance of that person working out is far better than someone coming in cold. So how can you get yourself recommended inside an organization? Networking!

Top ten networking tips

Here is my top ten list of networking tips.

1. Interested is interesting
2. Pay it forward
3. Be on time
4. Be prepared for your meetings
5. Ask for (and offer) personal introductions
6. Send thank-you notes

7. Deliver as promised
8. Keep excellent notes
9. Follow up with your contacts
10. Do more of what you do best

Interested is interesting

Networking is actually very simple if you remember this simple mantra: Interested is interesting. You may not realize it, but people like people who take a real interest in them. It is the charm of a marvelous listener … someone who asks you questions and seems genuinely interested in you. It is basic human nature to warm in that scenario. We live in such a fast-paced world, it doesn't happen often. So, just remember this: take a real interest in them (get curious like a 4-year old) and the conversation will be an easy one.

Often job hunters go into networking meetings nervous and worried about what to say, so they launch into talking about themselves …what they know best, what they want, and what they need. Well, it is not all about you. If you are particularly nervous about networking events, you may want to prepare a few questions you'd feel comfortable asking. Yes, chit-chat. "What brings you here today?" or "How did you hear about this event?" or "What do you do for fun in the winter?" Or, find an interesting news event to talk about … "Did you hear about …?" Let your personality shine. Ask questions about things you are interested in. No, you're not being fake. You're breaking the ice and starting a conversation. Be careful asking about things that are too personal. It can be dangerous ground.

Pay it forward!

This is the most important aspect of networking. Help others first. Go into every meeting (in person, over the phone, or even over email) with this attitude: "How can I help this person?"

If you approach each connection this way, two things will happen:

- You will start to feel good about asking for help because you are helping others as well. It is tough to ask for help (and you *must* ask for help during your job hunt!). Helping others makes it easier for you to ask for help.

- You will get your good will back tenfold. Those people who you help (recommend other connections, books, suggestions … whatever!) will think of you first, and often. As a result, your network will expand exponentially.

- Helping other people before you ask for help is the rule of reciprocity. If you help people, they will be inclined to return the favor. By helping others, you are making deposits in accounts from which you can withdraw later.

Many people look at me and say, "How can I help people right now? I am unemployed (overworked, miserable with my life, etc.). I have nothing to offer."Well, yes you do! When I say, "help," it can be as simple as sending someone a link to a web site or a copy of a relevant article on an issue they are struggling with. Introduce them to someone in your network who has something in common with them (professionally or personally).

The best way to help people is to ask them, "How can I help you?" You might get something as unexpected as, "You know, I am shopping for a new car and I'm thinking about a Jeep. If you know anyone who is driving one, I'd love to see what they think about it." The important thing is to cultivate a habit of being interested in the needs of others. Once you discover their needs, you are well on the way to finding a way that you can help.

Be on time!

Do I really have to say this? Yes, I do. I am stunned by the number of people who ask to meet with me and show up late. Or, show up late to a job interview. This is not just my pet peeve. I can assure you that people in your network and potential employers will be equally miffed (because they tell me as much). When I surveyed successful recruiters, this was among their chief complaints, and many recruiters said it immediately puts a candidate at the bottom of their list. That is not where you want to be. Of course, life gets in the way sometimes. You need to plan for the unexpected and leave early so you can be on time, in case you run across bad traffic or a detour. Nothing says, "You do not matter to me" or, "I am not really interested in you or this job" more than showing up late for a meeting. That is not a way to ask for and get help from someone. You need to be 5-10 minutes early for a meeting, **especially** if you requested it. If being on time is hard for you, leave 15 minutes early for every meeting. Make it happen. No excuses.

Be prepared for meetings

Once someone has agreed to meet with you, come prepared. It is helpful to write an agenda before you go to the meeting, complete with goals and questions to ask. I offer a sample below, but your agenda will vary depending upon the person you are meeting and the purpose of the meeting. Use this as a guide and make it your own.

Sample agenda for a networking meeting
Primary goals for call or meeting:

- Get an overview of _____'s career
- Find out why he likes what he does for a living.
- Ask about hobbies outside of work.
- Get suggestions for my job hunt (how to, where to, etc.).
- Get review of my marketing plan (reality check on what jobs I am going for, how much money I am asking for).
- Ask for referrals to other people who can help me.
- Uncover one way I can help _____ in his career.

    Questions to ask:

- How are you on time today?
- So how do you know _____?
- Where did you work before _____?
- Tell me a little bit about how you found your way to
    _____.
- Can you help me understand your role, those around you, what you're responsible for?

- May I share my resume and marketing plan with you and get your thoughts and suggestions?
- Do you know anyone who might be hiring in this space?
- Do you have a sense of the market salary range for the job I want?
- What can I do for you? How can I help you?
- Who else do you think I should talk to?
- Thank you very much for your time today!
- When should I follow up with you?

Ask for (and offer) personal introductions

I call these "warm referrals" versus "cold" ones. Make sure you reciprocate and do this for other people in your network as well! Ideally, when you get a referral, ask if that person will please send a quick email or make a phone call. A phone call is ideal ("Susan, I met someone today who I think you should meet.") If that feels like too much to ask, then ask the person to send an email (virtual) introduction.

One tip: do not sign anyone up for a face-to-face meeting. In other words, suggest that they connect—don't suggest they meet for lunch. Introduce them to each other and let them decide whether they want a face-to-face meeting or not.

Here are some examples of good, warm email introductions:

Sample Email Introduction #1:

> I'd like to introduce you to one another! I'll keep this brief as I've already bragged about each of you on the phone about the other, but here's a little context:
>
> Bob and I have known each other for 5+ years, and he's a cherished part of my network (and friend). He was formerly head of marketing/biz dev at ABC Company, and is coming up on 3 years as EVP of Sales, Marketing and Business Development for XYZ Corp (check them out at XYZ.com).
>
> Jane has launched her own unique enterprise, Soup to Nuts, in the last year, after extensive experience within leading corporations in the technology space. She's focusing on the intersection of technology and marketing, helping companies put the right people and processes in place who can bridge the gap between technology and marketing. And she is really good at it! (You should hear some of her turnaround stories.) I was just recently introduced to Jane, but the intro is from another, very trusted member of my network. I've cheated and attached the information about Soup to Nuts on this note.
>
> I hope you both find it worthwhile to connect.
>
>
> Michelle
>
> P.S. You both love to water-ski! **Sample Virtual Introduction #2:**

Nate and Tom, I think you'd both benefit from being in each other's network!

Nate used to lead marketing at TUB Company, and he's now President of the Bucket Company, where he has led absolutely explosive growth by every metric.

Tom has started his own unique search firm focusing on "doing it right" by medium-sized companies.

I know you are both busy people, but I suspect you are often looking for, or talking to, the same kinds of small and mid-sized companies who require both of your services.

I'll leave it to you all to connect - but thought I'd put the introduction out there.

Regards,

John

Sample Virtual Introduction #3:

Hello, you two. As you both know, I like to put smart people with similar interests together. So here you go! Rick, I know Jane from my Tubby Co. days. She is sharp, accomplished and fun. She just went through a lay-off (remember our lay-off from TUV Company?) and is looking for a role as a Director/VP Applications or PMO in a larger company or CIO role at a smaller company.

Jane, Rick just left BeeBeeBee and joined DeeDee Insurance as a Senior IS Director.

I hope you two manage to connect and see how you can help each other expand the network.

Keep well and have a wonderful weekend, you two!

Call me where I can help –

Robert

Sample Virtual Introduction #4:

Hello! I can't recall if I've introduced the two of you. If not, I am glad to finally do so!

Mike has a gift for translating technology into a consumer need (and even more powerfully--translating a need into a solution) and Catherine is well into launching her own search firm at the intersection of technology and marketing.

Mike, you may have some interesting leads for Catherine, who is looking for someone to fill this position (attached). Catherine, Mike is looking to make a job change and would really benefit from your wisdom and inspiration.

You both have 2 sons...in case you want some more random trivia.

Hope the connection is fruitful.

Jane Doe <u>janedoe@jandoe.com</u> [39] (111)111-1111

I hope these examples gave you an idea of just how easy it is to make introductions, spread goodwill, and get your network working for you.

Send "Thank you" notes—always!

Go get some thank-you cards you like. Put some of them in your car with stamps, in your planner with stamps, and at your desk at home with stamps. Why? So you can send a thank-you note immediately following a phone call or a meeting with someone who is trying to help you.

Email thank-you notes are good, but they are not great. I suggest you do both. Send a brief email and follow up with a handwritten "Thank you" note. You want to differentiate yourself? This is the best way. Ideally, you should send a handwritten note to everyone who helps you in any way.

Give credit where credit is due. One thing people want is a "thank you!" for their efforts.

Deliver as promised

If you promise to deliver something to someone (an introduction, an article, a book), good for you! Make sure you do it—within 1-2 days.

Keep excellent notes

Keep excellent notes about each person you talk with. These notes need to be accessible in a pinch (like when your phone rings and you are trying to remember details about the person on the other line). So, I suggest you keep a notebook you can take with you everywhere, as well as a contact manager (like Microsoft Outlook or ACT), for taking notes. Wherever you take notes, make sure they are all together and readily accessible.

Keep track of all the people you connect with, so you can reference them, thank them as you go along, and keep them posted. Either keep track of contacts on your contacts list or, if you are tech-savvy, you can make a note using a contact manager (like Microsoft Outlook), each time you are introduced to someone. Take special care of your champions (those who are really trying to help you) and keep them posted as you progress.

People who are new to networking often ask me, "Exactly what information should I gathering?"

Here are some suggestions:

- Full name, spelled correctly. (If the name is unusual, also spell it phonetically, the way you say it.)

- Full contact data (phone numbers, email address, mailing address).
- Referral. (How you were referred to this person.) Keep this information at the top of your notes on each person so you do not forget.
- Current employer and past employers (if you know them).
- Title.
- By date, your communication with this person.
- After each conversation, write a quick bulleted list of what you learned, what they are going to do for you, and what you are going to do for them:

    o REFERRED ME TO Joan Basket weaver
    o REFERRED ME TO Tyrone Lehman
    o I REFERRED Bob to Susan Jackson
    o I PROMISED to invite Bob to the Mt. Kilimanjaro networking event

- Capture any personal details (kids, hobbies, etc.). If someone cared enough to share them, you should care enough to remember them.

Here's an example of notes on a contact:

Contact: Tom Jones

In notes section:

SUE G REFERRAL vie email 06-06-08

6-7-08: Talked to Tom over phone. Tom is an administrative assistant. Wants to transfer his skills from finance to healthcare. Sharp, fun and has 2 kids 5 and 11. Loves snow skiing. I can't help him much, but I sent him on to Susie Que.

Tom referred me to Bobby Brown.

Connect the dots on who knows who.

If you find a power networker who keeps referring you to people (and you cannot keep track), I suggest a visual tool to help you. For example:

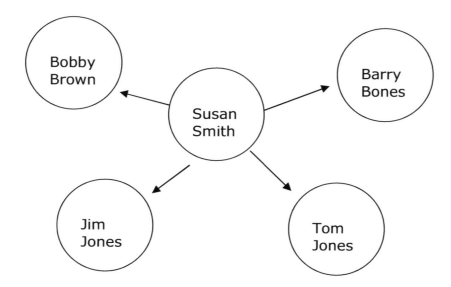

Top benefits to tracking all this information:

- Time management
- Reputation
- Staying in control
- Being prepared at all times

An illustration:

Tom just dropped his kids off at school and his phone rings. He answers it. It is the recruiter at his #1 target company. He applied for a job there. He also met someone who works for the company last week and spoke with her last week. He cannot remember who she is! He opens up his job hunt organizer and flips to his jobs section. Voila! There is the job he applied for, as well as notes about Susie Que. He is able to talk to the recruiter effectively about the job *and* mention his phone conversation with Susie Que. The call goes well. The recruiter schedules an in-person interview with Tom. In the meantime, the recruiter reaches out to Susie Que, who says Tom is stupendous for the job. Tom just went from #10 on the recruiter's list to #1.

You will benefit enormously from taking a few minutes to jot down notes on each person you meet. Once again, 80% of your job leads will come from networking, so nurture those people who are out there helping you.

Follow up regularly

Stay in front of your main networking contacts. You know ... the ones you think about regularly. Let them know you are thinking about them.

If a contact promises to deliver something to you (an email introduction, a lunch set up with someone), make note in your calendar to follow up three to five days later and see if they have had any luck with that. They may forget, and a gentle reminder with the name of the new connections will be helpful.

Here's an example:

> "Hello, Sue. Once again, it was great meeting you on Tuesday. Thank you for your time. You mentioned a referral to Bob Puppet and Sue Sand Dollar. Have you had a chance to connect with either of them? Is there anything else you need from me to facilitate these introductions?"

> Ideally, try to reciprocate as much as you can. If someone is making connections for you, what type of connections can you help them make? Often, you can help in ways outside of work. I recently met with someone who is starting to take care of elderly parents and is struggling. Because I have been going through that for three years now, I have a number of resources to share. I sent them off to him, making personal introductions via email where I felt it was appropriate.

Send periodic job hunt updates to your trusted network. Here is an example:

> **Email Subject: Career Search Update**

> "Hello! I just wanted to let you know that I'm still in the market for a new position as an IT Director at a small or mid-sized company. I've heard from several of you this past six weeks and do appreciate your time and consideration. I'm encouraged by the continued contacts and opportunities. Please keep them coming. As a reminder, an ideal contact for me is anyone who works in technology (IT). All it takes is that one connection. Here is a recap of my ideal opportunity:

> **IT Director or Leadership role.** My greatest strength is my ability to lead and inspire the business and IT to work together toward building a profitable business. I bring passion, expertise, and 15 years of skinned knees to the table."

> Thanks a lot!

> Joe

We all get busy with our lives. As much as someone might want to keep you top of mind, life just gets in the way. Help them remember you. Make it easy for them to remember what you want and what you offer. Do not assume, no matter how great your meeting was, that they will remember what you are looking for or anything beyond "I really liked Joe." Following up is a great way to remind them.

Do more of what you do best!

Do you know where you are at your best? Trust your gut on this; it never lies. Do you love meeting people and look forward to networking meetings? If so, chances are good that group meetings are well worth your time. On the other hand, if you feel ill every day you look at your calendar and see a networking meeting on it, you should take a hard look at whether or not those are worth your time. Furthermore if you dread such meetings, chances are good that you are not putting your best foot forward at them. I recommend you stay home and take time to schedule and conduct in-person meetings. Don't shut down networking events entirely. Just be judicious about which ones you attend. Or, take a friend with you.

- **Groups:** Are you great at meeting people in large groups? Fabulous! Then, do a lot of group meetings. If you stink at group meetings, focus on individual meetings and take a buddy with you to group meetings.

- **Written communication:** If you write well, send lots of written communications. If you do not write well, find someone to help you create some standard templates you can use and focus on phone calls or get out there and mingle in person.

- **Phone:** You need to call people during your hunt. You need to push yourself to make phone calls, even when you are nervous. That said, you may not do well over the phone. Write scripts. Be prepared (always have your job organizer with you). Try to talk to every single person who calls you—when they call you. You have their attention now, and if you don't take it, you may not get it again.

  Special note for the really nervous. Talk to the person for awhile, then ask if you can call them back a little later. Say something like, "I would love to talk to you. I am afraid now is not a great time. May I call you in 15 minutes? Half an hour?"

Where to Start Networking

- Make a list of people you know already
- Make a list of people you want to know
- Start calling and asking for help and face-to-face meetings
- Send out an email with your marketing plan and/or resume.
- Follow up immediately on referrals and leads

Make a list of people you know already

Pull out **Worksheet 18: Networking contacts**. Who do you know already? While you were building your target market, you probably thought of people you know who are in those roles, at those companies. If you are ready to talk, start calling them right now. If you have strong, trusted relationships with some of these people, ask them to help you brand and position yourself. Yes, ask for help! Meet them for coffee or lunch and review your background, your target market, and ask for their feedback on what makes you great, what your message should be, what your resume should capture. If you are still a little shaky on your communication, then wait—but not for too long!

People often say to me at this stage, "I don't really have a network." You *do* have a network! You will be amazed where your job leads are. Often, they are through your intimate personal network. If you are wondering, "Who should be part of my job hunt network?" The answer is, **"Everyone you know!"** My sister got a job lead at an espresso stand last week!

Professionally, think of past and present colleagues. Then think about people you know, perhaps from outside the company (for example, vendors and channel partners.) Personally, think about where you go in life (your neighbors, your friends, your church, your doctor, your dry cleaner).

Tips for calling people you already know:

- **Stretch.** Do not be shy. The more people you tell, the faster you will find what you are looking for. Remember, in our lifetime, everyone we know will be out of a job, or looking for one at least once and, more likely, several times. You are not alone. You have nothing to be ashamed of. And you will help others wherever you can. As you go, help others as much as you can. Keep filling up the piggy bank and it will come back to you in spades.

- **Make sure you spend time with your champions.** Supporters. Do not go to the naysayers (people who fill you with worry and give you reasons to doubt yourself) in your life. In fact, avoid those people at all costs during your job hunt. You need people who believe in you and encourage you. Get rid of these "deflators" in your life right now. Go for the positive relationships.

Make a list of people you want to know

Think about people you may *know of* at some companies and write them down. You may simply start with titles (VP of Finance, Snickerdoodle Inc.). You will add to this list as you research and continue your job hunt. You will take this list along with you to networking meetings and ask the person from that company, "Do you happen to know the VP of Finance at Snickerdoodle Inc.?"

Start calling—ask for help and face-to-face meetings

If you ask, you shall receive.

Sample introductory phone script:

> "Hello, _____.
> My name is _____.
> _____ suggested I give you a call.
> I am on the hunt for _____.
> _____thought you would be a good person for me to network with.
> Do you have a few minutes to talk?"

Send an email with your marketing plan and resume

"Hello, _____. I thought I would touch base with you. It's been awhile since we met at _____. I am on the hunt for a new job and want to know whether you have any ideas for me.

Here is what I am looking for:

I've attached my resume and marketing plan as an update. I would appreciate the chance to buy you a cup of coffee and reconnect. Do you have some time in the next week?

Joe Jones

111-111-1111

Follow up immediately on referrals and leads

Nothing impresses people more than getting an immediate, enthusiastic response. Even if you do not have time, make the time. All you need is one minute to respond by saying, "Hi. I'd love to connect. I'm running out to a meeting at the moment. What might be a good time for you in the next day or two?

Find a personal connection. If the person was referred to you, ask that person for some connecting points before you call (personal and professional).

For example:

- Works in the same industry as yours
- Works in the company you want to go work for
- Is a neighbor
- Also loves SCUBA diving
- Has children the same age as yours

If you cannot get any connecting points, try to find your own prior to your meeting. One way is to do a quick online search and see what you find out about that person. Pinpoint why you want to meet with this person and develop a brief agenda for your phone call and your eventual in-person meeting.

What to Say

I get questions every day like, "What do I say?" "How do I ask?" "How do I introduce myself?" Here are some tips and tricks to the art of communicating well during your job search.

Meeting someone for the first time:

Hello, _____. My name is _____. What do you do?"

Hello, _____. My name is _____. What do you do for fun?"

Notice I did not ask, "Where do you work?" If you are unemployed, it is especially helpful to avoid asking this question because it's a one-way street to being asked the same question. There is no better way to take a happy, casual introduction and make the other person say "Oh." There is no shame in being unemployed at all, but you just want to put that conversation off until you have established some rapport. In contrast, if you ask, "What do you do?" the other person will likely respond with what they do, and then ask you what you do. You can say easily and confidently what you do ... and *then* add that you are looking for something new at the moment.

Create drafts

Save time: When you develop your first message (this can wait until you need one), save it in a draft so you can reuse it. Then tweak it as necessary for individual situations. This is much easier than developing a message from scratch each time. I have draft emails sitting in (you guessed it!) my "drafts" folder. I simply copy and paste them into new emails and modify them as needed.

Letters of Introduction

Know who you are talking to and personalize your introduction. If you are about to write a "Dear Sir" letter, stop and ask yourself, "Why am I wasting any energy even sending it?" What do *you* do with mail you receive which is addressed to "Dear sir?" You throw it away! Don't bother sending notes that will get thrown away.

Be clear and concise in your communication

As you are networking, you want every person you talk to clearly aware of what you want and how they can help you. Spoon-feed them your 30-second pitch. Here is an example of a great first introduction.

Sample introduction - by referral

> Good afternoon Catherine,
>
> Betty Boop at ABC Company suggested I contact you. I am interested in a sales consultant or account management position and she thought you might be able to help me network.
>
> **My experience includes:**
>
> - 10 years of business to business sales experience with a variety of size companies
> - Repeated history of success prospecting, cultivating, and closing sales with human resource, occupational health and safety professionals
> - A consultative style that incorporates listening skills, problem solving, and connecting people to appropriate resources
> - Ability to develop and manage customer relationships
> - High energy and enthusiasm for interacting with a variety of people

Are you free in the next week or two to meet for coffee? My resume is attached.

Thank you for your consideration.

Susan Que

Groups and Associations

Local organizations, trade groups, user groups, networking groups and job transition groups all combine to make up a powerful network of people for you. With a little research and some deliberate outreach, you can get connected to the right people.

Do this early, as some of the most valuable groups in your network meet only once every two months. Furthermore, many are by invite only, and you will have to find someone to sponsor you.

How to find the right groups for you

- **Ask your network**. "What groups and associations do you belong to? Do you suggest I join? Are there any others you have heard of that I should look into?".

- **Search online.** Do Internet searches based upon your industry, functional area of expertise, and local market.

- **Look in the business section of your local newspaper**. Almost all newspapers (paper or online) list weekly business networking groups. Back to my earlier tip, "do more of what you do best." If you do well in groups, go to any group that looks interesting to you. You will be amazed at the connections you'll start to make. In the beginning, hit the networking groups hard, because they will force you to practice and hone your 30-second story.

In summary, joining and visiting local groups and associations can be a great way to network. The deeper you can go into a network that fits what you are looking for the better. There is power in numbers. In one hour at the right group event, you can meet 10-20 people compared to the hours spent driving around town to meet with people. You'll quickly identify some people you should get to know better and ask them to get together for a one-on-one. Additionally, many organizations post open jobs and can get you connected with the hiring managers directly.

Company Web Sites

Company web sites can be a valuable part of your job hunt. There are several ways to use them.

- **Researching** the company prior to networking meetings and job interviews.

- **Looking for job postings.** If there are particular companies that interest you (that made it on your target list), routinely visit their job postings (perhaps once a week). If companies post their jobs at all, the first place they usually put them is out on their own web site. Keep in mind that many jobs never make it to the web site, so you still have a better chance if you network in. However, looking at what is posted will give you an idea of opportunities that are available, as well as what required skills and experience companies are looking for. It is critical to understand what your target market is asking for, so you can package your skills & expertise in a language they can understand. Do exercise this for your top five target companies only. Remember, you need to limit your time online.

- **Discovering company lingo**, desired skills, if you are having an informational interview. If you get a lead for a job through your network and now have an opportunity to apply for a job that is not on the company's web site, you can often find similar jobs on the company's web site that will help you tailor your resume and prepare for your interview.

Work Smart Online

Ahhhh. The allure of the Internet. Depending on how you approach it, **the Internet can be your friend or your enemy** during your job hunt. When used correctly, it can be an invaluable piece of your job hunt strategy. It can be a wealth of information, connections and inspiration. You might even find your dream job on the Internet. However, when used incorrectly, it can actually stand in the way of you getting a job. You must be deliberate in how and when you use the Internet.

What the Internet is great for:

- Research
- Finding and connecting with people (especially through professional and social networking sites)
- Information on job hunting (tips, tricks, articles)
- A *little* bit of job hunting (finding jobs)

What the Internet is not great for:

- Finding jobs.
- The job boards are seductive. They are enticing. They are chock full of tools and tips to keep you out on them. They will steal your precious time. Yes, of course you need to spend *some* of your time on job boards. However, if you are not careful, you will discover that an entire day has been wasted surfing the World Wide Web.
- Many jobs never get posted online. Why? Time and money. The big job boards are expensive and smaller companies cannot afford to use them. Smaller job boards, especially niche ones, can be great for companies. The problem is that they often do not have the time or in-house expertise to find these niche sites and post jobs with them. So, your dream job may never even hit the Internet.
- Applying for jobs.

The average company uses the Internet to hire 10% to 20% of its employees

That means that you have a 10%-20% chance of finding your next job on the Internet.

Companies want you in their database, *just in case* you are the right fit for them one day. You need to jump through extensive hoops to apply online with them, all in the hopes that they might have a good job for you someday. Good for them, but not good for you. Of course, you would like them to call you down the road, but your time is better spent elsewhere. Do not let them steal this time away from you, unless you are facing one of these situations:

- You are applying for a specific job and you are really well qualified for the job. Ideally, use your network to find out more about that position before you waste one minute applying online.
- The company is on your top five list and you really want to work for them.

A testimonial on the Internet as a black hole:

"I read articles, I heard the statistics (65% of people find jobs through people they know, only 5-15% find job through the Internet), but I thought I knew better. I told myself, 'I have no network. I've been working too hard the last four years. I don't know anyone and nobody really wants to help me, so why bother asking?' So, I wasted two months chasing opportunities on the Internet. I felt productive! I was getting interviews! But they always fell apart. Finally, I realized that the job interviews I was going on were not solid, they were extremely competitive, and they were wasting my time! I started networking and realized that I *did* know people. Incredibly, within three days, I found a job opportunity through my network. It was perfect for me and I started the new job three weeks later!"

How to use the Internet in your job hunt

Spend no more than 20% of your time on the Internet.

Be deliberate. The Internet is a treasure-trove of information, ideas, jobs, and connections. It can also be the Bermuda triangle (you will get lost out there, never to be found again). You must be very deliberate about how and when you use the Internet. You must ask yourself, each and every time you flip to a new page on the Internet, **"Is this worth my time? Is what I am doing, or reading, getting me closer to a great new job?"**

How to behave on the Internet (web etiquette)

You and only you are responsible for your personal and professional image online. You are in control of most, but not all, of that. So, the first order of business is to conduct yourself well. The other order of business is to make sure your personal and professional acquaintances are conducting themselves well.

Employers are checking these sites for information on you. They are doing Google searches. They are looking you up on Facebook and LinkedIn, so make sure you know what's out there.

Some tips on web etiquette:

- Respond quickly and graciously to everyone who reaches out to you by name. You will hear from many people who are trying to help, sending you jobs that are not a fit. You need to respond quickly and appreciatively, no matter how off the mark these people are. This will give you an opportunity to help them understand what a great fit is for you, as well as a chance to thank them for their efforts. If you have an 80% chance of getting a job through your network, then you must take care of that network. However, if you get an anonymous request, you need not respond to those.

- Be professional!
- Manage your online presence

Biggest online blunders:

- **Using unprofessional online names**
  Email addresses such as Bubba@hotmail.com or Cutie@msn.net, or fishingfiend@abc.com are not appropriate for a job hunt, These types of email addresses will give people a negative impression of you. Take the time to set up a professional email address. The safest email address is firstnamelastname@domainname or some variation of that. For example, johndoe@msn.com. If you do not have email account, you can set one up easily at msn.com, gmail.com, or yahoo.com, among others.

- **Getting too personal**
  If your friend has pictures posted of you at a party last weekend and there are some photos you would not like to share with a potential employer, ask your friend to take those photos of you down.

- **Being careless in chat rooms, blogs, etc.**
  Where you go and what you say online can come back to haunt you. Aside from social networking sites, this also means be careful in chat rooms. Never say something online that you would not want repeated to a potential employer. For example, there are chat rooms where disgruntled employees post complaints about their employers. Do not go there!

Search the Internet for your name and see what pops up. You might be amazed at what you find. So, also, might a prospective employer. For instance, if you recently got a DUI, you may be surprised to know that it is listed on the World Wide Web. Don't be surprised if someone interviewing you has discovered the same thing. Once again, the more prepared you are for what may come your way, the more equipped you will be to handle it. Control what you can control, and be prepared for the rest.

Be careful where you go. Things can quickly get crazy online. Predators are on the prowl, so be smart about where you go and where you post your information on the World Wide Web.

Two important aspects of Internet usage

- How and when to use the Internet
- How to behave on the Internet

How and when to use the Internet

Here you'll find information about various types of web sites and how to maximize your use of them. The web sites mentioned here are distinctly different and of varying value, depending on what you want, your market, and how well maintained they are. All of those things are subject to change.

The most valuable types of sites in your job search are:

- Social networking sites
- Professional networking sites
- Groups and associations
- Niche sites

Social networking sites

Social networking sites are taking off like wildfire, and it can be great fun to reconnect with past schoolmates, colleagues, and friends. Just remember, however, that social and professional are closely linked. Employers are often doing Internet searches on potential hires. That means those pictures of you drinking at a party in college might just show up. Is that the reputation you want being put forward during a job hunt? Hopefully not. Make sure that you, and everyone you know, keeps your reputation intact online. If you are not already on the purely social networking sites, I would stay off of them for now. Connect only with people you know and trust; "archive" the other invitations. If you are already on, make sure you check your profile regularly to make sure there are no pictures or stories you do not want a potential employer to see. If you discover a photo you want removed, ask the person very nicely to remove it.

Just because you are out on LinkedIn does not mean you are job hunting.

Many people say to me, "I cannot go on those social networking sites because it means I am job-hunting." Yes you can, and you need to. If your boss says, "I saw you out on LinkedIn. Are you leaving us?" You can say, "Well, are *you* leaving us? What were you doing out there?" and smile. Seriously, though, the message is as simple as, "I kept hearing from people that I needed to go out there and start networking online, so I finally listened. It's a powerful resource and I am already getting ideas for our business from it."

"You are judged by the company you keep."

At the tender age of 14, my father said this to me. I did not like hearing this message then ("How depressing!" I thought) and, even now, I don't like thinking about it. But it is so true. Just be thoughtful about who you connect with, how you represent yourself, and what you say online. It becomes a permanent record. Truly. Perception is 9/10 of the law.

How you can put social networking sites to work for you

- **Be selective.** Find two social networking sites (like LinkedIn) and sign up.

- **Focus on what you bring to the table.** Networking sites are for your personal profile, not your company's profile. Your online profile really is *all about you.*

- **Build your profile.** Use your resume and what you want as a guide. Populate your profiles on each site with the key aspects of your professional life. Think about your value and what makes you unique. Do not put your entire resume out there. Include a link to it, if you like. Think of each online profile as a 60-second commercial about you. This may sound daunting, but with the work you have already done in the 4-step process, this will not be a challenge—and it will pay off tenfold! Past colleagues and friends will find you based upon your past employment, college, and high school. And they are people who will want to help you in your search.

- **Upload a picture.** Use a recent professional photo. People expect to see a picture. You do not need to pay a professional to take one, but make sure yours is professional. A picture with your cat is only cute if you are a veterinarian.

- **Be relevant.** If you took a class in underwater basket weaving, but want to expand your network in finance, leave the underwater basket weaving out.

- **Recommend professional web sites:** You can post your personal web site—if it is professional. Your employer's site is helpful. This is not the place to recommend your favorite site on skiing.

- **Check your contact settings.** Use these settings to tell people what type of connections you would like to make. If you are employed and worried about your employer accusing you of looking for a new job, simply leave that box unmarked.

Professional networking sites

Networking sites come in all shapes and sizes, from social to professional. They are valuable, but again you will need to watch your time spent on these sites.

- Find two professional networking sites you like and sign up.
- Find two user groups that fit your skills and sign up. Many of them are informal places for candidates to post their resumes and for companies to post their jobs.

Job boards

In their simplest form, "Job boards" (or job search engines) are web sites that allow employers and job hunters to find each other. They have grown tremendously since their inception in the early 1990s, and they offer a host of services to the employer and the job seeker. At minimum, employers post their job openings and job seekers post their resumes. At maximum, they allow employers and job seekers to track their conversations with each other and give employers powerful ways to sort and rank candidates against each other. Job boards are usually free for job seekers, although there are some exceptions (generally, in the realm of upper management and executive jobs). They range in size and reach from major, large-scale generalist boards to small niche job boards (for categories such as engineering, technology, legal, insurance, finance, teaching and seasonal jobs).

If job boards are new to you, take a quick peek (and I mean quick!) at these job boards:

- www.careerbuilder.com

- www.hotjobs.com
- www.monster.com
- www.usajobs.gov

Remember: *You have a 10-20% chance of finding your dream job out on job boards, so* **watch the clock!**

Things you should know and understand about job boards:

- **Job boards get paid to support employers, not job seekers** (except for a small minority). They certainly try to attract you, but always keep in mind that they are there to serve the employer.

- **The big job boards are expensive for employers**, so the good job for you may not be posted out on those sites. And if it is posted on a job site, it is likely only posted on one of the big boards.

- **Job boards are highly competitive.** Thousands of people see the job postings and you are competing against every one of them—blind.

- **If you apply online, take time to do it the right way.** You must make sure you use as many keywords as you can on your resume. Your resume is being sorted along with every other applicant, by software, by "keyword relevance." This is powerful technology for employers, but it can greatly reduce your chances of being selected unless you modify your resume to fit each position you apply for, based upon the required and desired skills. If you do not tailor your resume for each position, it is probably a waste of time to apply online for it.

- **Most employers searching resumes search only on resumes posted within the last 30 days.** So, if your resume had not been touched in more than 30 days, employers will likely not find you

Work smart when using job boards

- Pick five boards (three major, two niche or specialty). Now, run a quick job search on these sites based on what you want and make sure they have the right kinds of jobs for you.
- Post your resume on those five sites.
- Be clear and concise about what you want.
- Set up "job agents" on these job boards to push jobs your way. You set the criteria and the boards send you jobs that match your desired criteria.
- Tweak your criteria once you start seeing jobs and understand that either too many or too few jobs are coming your way.
- Once you see a position that really interests you, go to your network for contacts inside that company. Preferably, first, see if you can get connected through your network. If not, apply online.
- Only apply for jobs for which you have 80% of the required skills.
- If you are gainfully employed during your job hunt, consider posting confidentially.
- Delete any job invitations that come to your confidential resume that are not a fit for you. If the sender does not know who you are, they won't know you have deleted it. This will save time for you and the person who sent it to you.
- Refresh your resume often (at minimum, every 30 days).

"Can't I just apply for jobs that interest me, and see what happens?"

If you see a job you want, but you know you're not really qualified (you don't have at least eight of 10 required skills), **do not apply** for it! No good will come of it. You may think "Oh, I am a fit for that position. I can do that job. I want that job. Maybe they'll see how great I am and overlook the required skills that I do not have." This will not happen online. This *might* happen in person, through a personal referral from someone in your network. Without a personal referral, however, your resume will hit the **"No way"** pile, and it might even damage your credibility. The recruiter or hiring manager may think, "He obviously cannot read a job requirement." Or, "How else would she stretch the truth if we hired her?" People do not want to help you if you apply for positions you are not qualified for. If you clearly only have five out of 10 required job skills, you are not qualified. Do not apply. It will hurt your reputation and irritate the recruiter or hiring manager. Your time is worth more than that! If you have 80% of what the job requires and you know you are a superstar in the other arenas, perhaps you should apply. But even that is a stretch.

Now go back to networking!

Trade and Business Publications

It is a good idea to be well read in your industry, especially while you are on the hunt for something new. It will help you connect, help you prepare for interviews, and help you be picky about where you go to interview. Very often, you will find articles written by industry leaders. If you find someone who looks like a good connection for you, you have an opportunity to reach out than to say, "I read your article and was intrigued by what you had to say. May I buy you a cup of coffee to learn more?" or something like that.

An excellent resource, if it is in your market, is the local Business Journal.

Work Smart with Recruiters

The right recruiter can be a tremendous asset to you in your search. The wrong one can be a huge drain on your time and your self-esteem. Five to fifteen percent of you get hired through recruiting firms and staffing agencies, so this avenue should not be ignored. However, like all aspects of this journey, you need to make sure you are talking to the right recruiters, and understand what they can and cannot do for you.

Recruiters can be valuable. Make sure the time you spend talking to recruiters is valuable time. Every conversation is an interview and an opportunity, so treat it that way. Unlike the Internet, where information is so broad and often far off the mark for you, your skills, and your market, recruiters have their finger on the pulse of what is happening in your space right now. Today. Feedback from the right recruiters in your local market can be the best information you get about your industry and your market. However, you can also waste a tremendous amount of time talking to the wrong recruiters, meeting with recruiters who will never have the right job for you, or expecting too much from recruiters.

Recruiters get paid to fill jobs. They do not get paid to help people find jobs. This means that they can only afford to spend time with and help people who appear to be a really good fit for the jobs they have that day. There are simply not enough hours in the day to help people the way they want to. So, although many of them would love to help you, they simply cannot afford to.

It is important to understand the job of a recruiter.

What recruiters do

- Fill jobs for their clients
- Scout for talent and keep the pipeline full by constantly networking
- Screen and select candidates according to job openings
- Influence the process
- Make the offers

A recruiter's clients are hiring managers, not candidates. As much as you would like recruiters to go find you a job, that is not what they get paid to do. Furthermore, even if they wanted to help you in that way (and many of them wish they had the time to help more people), they simple do not have the time. Unfortunately, they get buried with so many candidates who *are* a fit, it is tough to spend any free time helping people who do not fit the jobs on their desk.

What recruiters do not do

- Find people jobs
- Write resumes
- Chart career paths
- Define the jobs they are filling
- Make final hiring decisions

Once again, as much as many recruiters would like to review your resume and help you rewrite it, they simply do not have the time to do so—unless you are a great fit for a job they have open today.

Types of recruiters

- Corporate, HR generalists
- Corporate, specialized
- Agency, generalist
- Agency, specialist
- Search firm, contingent
- Search firm, retained

How recruiters get measured

This varies from company to company, and from internal to agency and search, but generally recruiters are measured by:

- Customer service with hiring managers
- Quantity (number of resumes submitted and jobs filled)
- Quality (right "fit" for the job)

- Time to fill
- Cost per hire or revenue generated (internal versus external)
- Turnover

Where recruiters are great

- Once you are in their database, recruiters will find you and call you if they have the right opportunity on their desk for you. So do send your resume if they ask you to, especially if that recruiter is in your area of expertise.

- Once you are interviewing with a recruiter, she can offer you real-time market information! Nobody has a better view of the market and industry, including salary and trends in hiring, than a seasoned recruiter who specializes in your field. She sees a broad cross-section of the market every day. She talks to clients and candidates, and is the first to see changes in the market. She has their finger on the pulse of what you need to know.

Where recruiters can drag you down

They may not understand what you do - at all!

Did you know that many recruiters, especially inside companies, work open positions across many functional areas? That means jack of all, master of none. They may be great at the internal process of hiring, but they are not great at understanding, functionally, what you do or how to put your best foot forward to hiring managers. In fact, they can inadvertently put your worst foot forward. I do not tell you this to scare you, but to remind you that you must never assume. Be clear and concise. Follow up a conversation with a recruiter with a nice, concise summary of why you think you're a great fit for the position.

They might waste your time

Recruiters will sometimes waste your time by keeping you "warm" when they have little or no chance of placing you. This is especially true of agency recruiters. Their job is to keep their pipeline full and keep you motivated to work with them. In doing so, candidates can easily walk away from a conversation feeling "Wow, Amy is going to find a new job for me. She said I fit right into their area of specialty, I have great skills and will be easy to place." That's great, but Amy must work on the jobs she has in hand. She has very little time to go looking for new jobs. So why do recruiters mislead people?

First, most recruiters are in the business because they love helping people, and they want to help you. They really have your best interest at heart. However, they get caught up in the romance of it and the hope that they come across the right job for you. Second, recruiters must keep their database full. In fact, agency recruiters are often measured by the number of people in their databases. They live in the world of "what-if" and each time they connect with a candidate, they know there is a chance they might have the right job for you one day. So they are nice, they are encouraging, and they want to take care of you. So, they may give you a sense of false hope. Don't let that lead you to forget that only five to fifteen percent of placements are made through outside recruiters. They *might* get the right job for you, but you cannot sit around hoping that happens.

What recruiters want from you

I conducted a recent survey to bring you the best tips for working successfully with recruiters. I asked this simple question: "What should a candidate do to get on the top of your pile?" These are the top 8 things that will make you a great candidate to work with:

- Know what you want, clearly and concisely
- Know what you've got to offer, for the job at hand (keep it simple)
- Be responsive (the early bird really does get the worm!)
- Be professional (keep negative comments about previous employers quiet)
- Be honest (do not ever stretch the truth)
- Be positive and enthusiastic (recruiters respond just as you do to positive people)
- Be coachable (recruiters can offer excellent advice, so be open to it)
- Know where you have applied (which companies, and how)

If you abide by these suggestions, you will be a pleasure to work with and, in return, so will the recruiters. Even though they get paid by the hiring manager, that does not mean they are not interested in helping you get what you want as well. Great recruiters know that if they do not get the candidates what they want, the candidates will not take the job. So a recruiter is definitely digging in to find out what is going to work for both parties, hopefully uncovering your motivators and desires. But they are not there to help you find a new job.

How to work with recruiters

Find the right recruiters. Be strategic.

- Research and get a list of the 10 recruiting or search firms in your market, in your industry.

- Ask your network which recruiters they recommend.

- Call (don't email) those recruiters and ask them what their specialty is, where the bulk of their placements were in the last six months. "I just want to see if I am the right fit for your business because I do not want to waste your time or mine." If a recruiter does not mention your area of specialty in the first one to three top placements, move on. Be gracious and send your resume if they ask (there is a slim chance they might come across an opportunity for you), but do not go meet with that recruiter. And do not keep calling or emailing that recruiter.

Be professional

For some reason, people get comfortable (way too comfortable!) with recruiters. You must remember that recruiters are an extension of the hiring manager. So, if you show up late, wear jeans, share personal information about yourself or others, you may as well be telling the hiring manager. Recruiters are easy to talk to. They are, in fact, in sales. Do not forget where their paycheck comes from, where their loyalties must lie. If you show up late for your interview with them, they assume you will do the same for their hiring manager now and once you are on the job. The recruiter's responsibility is to submit the **best** candidate for the job, and "best" is not simply about skills. Never, ever bad-mouth former employers.

No matter how poorly you were treated. Only you will look bad when you speak negatively about people or companies.

Be responsive!

Time is money, especially around hiring. The **early bird really does get the worm**. Agency recruiters usually have only one or two days to present candidates. Corporate recruiters end up moving on the first candidates who respond. That is simply the way it goes. So, the minute you get a voicemail from a recruiter, call him back! Even if you cannot talk for long, call to say, "Thank you so much for your interest, I am not available today. Can we set a time to talk tomorrow?"

Be brief!

Because recruiters have so many applicants, and/or so many positions on their plate, it is essential that you are clear and concise in describing what you want, in your answers to their questions, etc. If you make it easy for them to understand who you are and what you want, you will either jump to the top of the list, or get eliminated sooner. Wouldn't it be nice to know sooner rather than later that you are not a fit for a particular job?

Here's an example of an outline for an email introduction to a recruiter:

> Hello, _____. I am on the hunt for a new job and thought I should reach out to you to see if I fit your typical candidate profile.
>
> Next, write one or two sentences that offer a career summary, only as it pertains to the job you want and think the recruiter might have. Keep it to one or two sentences and make sure you highlight what you think the recruiter hires for:
>
> - Brief rundown on your target roles, job titles
> - Two to three career highlights – again, as they pertain to your audience
> - Best way to reach you if they are interested (cell, email, home phone)
>
> Thank you very much for your time. I look forward to connecting soon.
>
> (You name)
>
> (Your contact details)
>
> Attach your resume

Ask for feedback! (on your resume, compensation, interviewing skills)

Ask how you can help them!

> "What searches are you working on right now? Maybe I can help you find some candidates." The act of reciprocity works as well with recruiters as with everyone else.

Send "thank you" notes!

Questions you can ask recruiters

Remember that each recruiter you meet might have your dream job sitting in the palm of his or her hand, so treat each conversation with the same level of respect and focus. Each conversation, no matter how formal or informal, is an interview.

However, your chances are getting hired range dramatically depending on the type of recruiter, the sales person for the job (if it is an agency), the employer, and the hiring manager. Many variables are out of your control. What you can control, however, is your understanding of the situation so you know how much energy to spend on each job opening.

Some questions you can ask to determine your chances

To determine the type of recruiter and area of expertise (does this recruiter understand what I do for a living?), you can ask these questions:

- What is your area of specialty?
- Where does the majority of your business come from?

To determine the strength of the relationship with the hiring manager, you can ask these questions:

- How did your firm get chosen to work on this job opening?
- Please describe the submission and interviewing process.
- What are the two must-have skills for this position?
- Why is this position open?
- Why have they rejected previous candidates?

To determine how competitive it is, you can ask these questions:

- How do I compare to other candidates for this job?
- Aside from working with you, do you know what else the client is doing to fill this?

To determine whether this is worth your time, you can ask these questions:

- Who is an ideal candidate for this position?
- How do I compare to other candidates for this job?
- How long has this been open?

One last tip about working with recruiters

Do not view recruiters as your enemy! I hear a lot of job hunters say bad things about recruiters because they feel they have been treated badly. This is an unfortunate side of the business. Typically, it is the result of poor communication and a lack of understanding on both sides. People say, "Recruiters strung me along" or, "He did not find me a job and he said he would." In all my years in this business, I can only name a handful of recruiters who really were dishonorable. Most are doing their very best to manage expectations on both sides and put the right people together at the right time. So don't think of them as your enemies. They are simply trying to do their job as best they can.

Remember: Recruiters are not there to help you find your next job. Corporate recruiters, agency recruiters, and headhunters are all paid by hiring companies. So, that is where their priority is and needs to be.

Job Fairs

Do some research in your area of specialty to find out whether job fairs are worth your time or not. They are last on the list because your time is generally better spent elsewhere. However, if you are good in groups and happen to be in an industry that uses them a lot (like pharmaceutical sales and nursing), you should definitely consider attending them.

Communicate Clearly

Of course, you know it is important to communicate well during your job search. The question is "How?" I get questions every day like, "What should I say?" and, "How should I say it?" This section is designed to help you know what to say. It is full of examples to follow and tailor to your own situation and personality.

Save time

Save time by creating online communications in draft format, so you have a template that you can tailor for each new recipient.

Know your audience

Learn as much as you can about the person you are addressing and tailor your letter as best you can. If you are networking well, you will use referrals for most of your communications. That means you should know your audience. When someone tells you, "Oh, you should call Bob Barker!" ask your friend why. Ask for specifics. "Why do you think I should call Bob? What do you think he can do for me? What do you think I might be able to do for Bob? Can you tell me anything about him that will help me connect—about his background, his family, his hobbies? What made you think I should call him?"

If you do not know who your audience is (you do not even have a name), you should skip it. A "dear sir" letter is a waste of your time. Unless you are going to deliver it on rollerblades singing the national anthem, it will go in the "Oh, that's nice" pile, never to be seen again. So, do not bother. What do you do with mail you get that is addresses to "Dear sir?" You throw it away!

Be specific

You need to be as clear and concise with people who know you as you are with people who don't know you. People need to know how to help you, so the more specific you can be (the more you spoon feed them), the more great connections and opportunities you will find.

Less is more. Do not share everything. Nobody needs to know you were laid off, lost your job, were downsized, whatever. That is simply too much information for an introduction. And it could hurt you. Simply state that you are looking and describe briefly what you are looking for. It is the nasty truth that people make assumptions, quickly. If you announce "Hi! I just got let go, and need a new job," people will automatically think "Oh, gee, I am not sure I should put this person into my network until I know why he was let go." Just keep it focused on what you want, not why. Keep it positive. Do not set yourself up to talk your way out of a corner.

"No thank you" notes

Yes, you need to send nice "no, thank you" notes and treat people well when they call or offer you a bad job via email. You *will* get invitations to look at jobs that are not a fit for you. You *will* get connected with people who will be no help to you in your search at all. If they know you by name (and not through a confidential resume), you need to treat these people well. They may not have the right job for you today, but they may tomorrow. And if you are professional and appreciative (yes, even when they are totally off the mark with what they send you!), they just might forward you on to someone who can help you. Never underestimate the power of one person to push you to the right connections. And never underestimate how we are all connected. That person you just met might be the next door neighbor of the CEO of your dream company.

Here's an example:

> A rookie recruiter at a large firm, who has no idea what he is doing, calls you about a job that is a total misfit for you. You are nice and say, "No, thank you" gracefully. That recruiter feels a little silly. She was impressed with you. She may very well walk down the hall to a senior recruiter and say, "Joe, this guy is not a fit for anything I have, but I know you work on a lot of senior positions. Will you take a look at him?" Do you want to meet him?"

Here is an alternative:

> You are rude to that rookie recruiter because she sent you a job that is way off the mark. The next week, you connect with a more seasoned recruiter at the same company who has the perfect job for you and asks the right questions. It seems terrific until the seasoned recruiter mentions your name in the weekly staff meeting. Rookie recruiter says, "Whoa. That guy is a *jerk*. Don't present him to your client. You said your client needs someone who can handle delicate political situations. This guy could be a bull in a china shop."

Apply with Panache

So, what do I mean by "apply with panache?" Make sure you stand out from the herd. Yes, you can do something different and creative (just keep it professional)! If, for example, you are a florist and you are applying at a new company, why not send a little portfolio of your most impressive flower arrangements? I do not recommend dropping by the company unsolicited, unless it is a small company or you are a door-to-door salesperson. People are busy and may or may not respond well to the interruption. But certainly, you can drop off a portfolio or a resume if you are in the neighborhood. So much depends on the company, your role, and your target audience. Feel free to think outside the box.

Putting your best foot forward is just as important when you apply for a job as it is when you interview for one. It takes time (hence, my emphasis throughout this book on only applying for jobs that fit you and your skills), but it is well worth it. In fact, if you do not take the time to tailor your resume and cover letter for a position, you may as well not apply (especially not online).

At minimum, you must make sure your resume reflects all the required skills, in terms your audience can understand. Speak their language. Corporate recruiters simply do not have time to call you and ask, "Do you have this skill?" So they call the candidates who have all the skills on their resume and they never get beyond that. Why? Several of *those* candidates stand out as good fits based upon their resumes.

Show clearly how your skills and expertise map to the required and desired skills. Focus on the results—what you can help this new company accomplish. Any easy way to keep your messages in check is to ask yourself "So what? Why should they care?"

Tailor your response as well as you can. Basically, breathe life into your resume with a cover letter by telling people why you are a good fit.

Here are some examples:

You need someone to lead and develop a small team of administrators.

In my last role as office manager, I managed four administrators. I reduced turnover by 28%, reduced the contingent staff by 35% and groomed two team members for promotions into other areas.

You need to drive business process improvement.

In my last role, I developed a five-question survey that my administrators used each time they took on a new project from employees. Customer satisfaction increased by 45% and my team's rework was significantly reduced.

"How do I handle all jobs that come to me, but not waste my time?"

When jobs come to you and you are interested, stop and ask yourself:

- Does the job fit what I really want?
- Do I have at least 80% of the required skills listed?
- If yes, and you are interested, first go to your network and see if you can find someone inside that company to introduce you to the right person.
- If you don't find a referral, call the company and ask to speak with the head of whatever department you're trying to get into (Marketing, Sales, and Customer Service).
- If all of this fails, apply online—but only if you are really excited about it and you are qualified for it (have 80% of required skills). If you have a major gap, do not apply!

Interview with a Bang

"There are no secrets to success. It is the result of preparation, hard work, and learning from failure."

— Colin Powell

Before we start this chapter, I want you to know that you should expect to go on a lot of interviews. It is difficult to find the right spot over the phone. In-person interviews are critical for you *and* the hiring manager to figure out if there is a fit.

You must assume (during each and every interview) that you want the job, and interview accordingly. Even if you have reservations, you must interview like this is your dream job and go for gold in the interview. Even if you think a potential interview or job might be a waste of your time, you must approach it with the same gusto as those you think are more important. Why?

First, during the interview, you may realize that, actually, this is a great opportunity or job potential. If you go in half-heartedly, it will be too late to recover and become their number one candidate.

Second, even if this job is not the right one for you, chances are the interviewer knows of another opportunity. If you go in with your "A-game," the interviewer will know how terrific you are and enthusiastically refer you on to someone who has the right connection or job for you.

I see this happen, much too often. It is very sad. People go in to meet with people about a job they don't think they want. They call it a "practice interview" and a "look-see." That's fine, but remember this: you might discover that, in fact, *this is your dream job*. Uh-oh. If you go in with your arms crossed (emotionally or physically), as though this is not an important interview, guess what? You are unprepared, unenthusiastic, **and it shows**. You will not be the top candidate. It is very tough to recover from this. So don't do it.

Are you nervous about interviewing? Let me tell you a little-known secret. The person interviewing you **wants you to be the one!** You need to know that, going in, very often the job is yours to lose! By the time you are interviewing, you are already one of the top three to five candidates. Furthermore, as the recruiter and hiring manager prepare for an interview (*if* they prepare!), they are saying to themselves, "I really hope this is the one." Nobody wants to waste their time interviewing 10+ people.

Remember: *As you walk into an interview, the person you meet is **very hopeful**. He or she wants you to interview well. Wants you to be the one!*

Let's keep this interviewing thing simple, because it actually is.

Basically, there are three things each interviewer wants to know about you:

1 Can you do the job?
2 Do you want the job?
3 Will you fit in with the team?

Top 10 tips for interviewing success

1. Dress the part.
2. Prepare.
3. Take care of your body and mind.
4. Give a firm handshake.
5. Be professional, yet touchable.
6. Let the interviewer drive.
7. Close the deal.
8. Say "thank you."
9. Debrief.
10. Follow up.

Follow these top 10 tips, and you'll be sure to interview with a bang—every time.

Dress the part

There is no excuse for wrinkled shirts, scuffed shoes, or ruffled hair. People do make quick judgments. Do not let something as silly as your appearance stand in the way of you making a great first impression. Dressing well delivers two messages.

1 "I appreciate you taking the time to meet with me and I care about this meeting."

2 "I am credible and respect myself enough to look professional."

Dress matters. Yes, business environments have become more casual in recent years. But do not assume that means you can dress down for an interview. People who dress well for interviews get farther along in the process than people who don't. Of course, there are rare exceptions. But why take a chance? The basic rule of thumb is to dress one level up from the person you are meeting. Not sure what to wear? Try asking the person who got you the interview. If you can't find anyone to tell you what the dress code is, err on the side of caution and dress up. If you are overdressed, you can laugh about it. If you are underdressed, the person who gets the job will be laughing about it. No, you do not have to go spend a fortune on a new navy blue suit. Just make sure you wear a jacket. For men, tie is optional (unless you are a manager or above). For women, pants are acceptable, as long as they are dress pants. Iron your clothes. Polish your shoes. Get a fresh haircut. Of course there are exceptions and you may want to argue with me about this. I am just telling you what I have seen over and over during my many years in this business. Well-dressed candidates pop to the top much faster than poorly-dressed candidates.

I would like to make one side comment about dressing for success. If 70-80% of people find new jobs through networking, the one connection you need might be in line in front of you at the grocery store. Do you want to be caught in your sweatpants feeling unprofessional? Probably not. I recommend you make sure you look and feel good wherever you go, especially if you are unemployed and anxious to find a job right away. I am honestly amazed at how unprofessional some people look when they come to networking events and job support groups. Yes, job support groups are often free and hosted by churches, but these are also the places where you'll find the connections you need. If someone is going to put his or her reputation on the line for you, he or she will think twice about it if you look really disheveled. People are more inclined to make connections for people they know will present themselves professionally. Just keep it simple, and always dress well so you feel good and can always make a great first impression. No, you do not need to go to the gas station in a suit. But you might want to rethink wearing jeans and sweatpants or sweatshirts.

Prepare

"To be prepared is half the victory."
- Miguel De Cervantes

The best interviewees think quickly on their feet and come up with smart, insightful answers. But very few can do that without a lot of preparation and some practice. For most of us, interviewing is like getting up on stage to perform. It takes practice. So start practicing! Set up informational interviews. Ask a friend to role play with you. If the idea of doing this makes your stomach roll, you *know* you must practice (because chances are good that without practice, you will do poorly in the interview that really matters). Let's face it. Interviewing is difficult. It is nerve-wracking, and you cannot know what to expect most of the time until you are in the middle of it. Like anything in life, if you prepare for what *might* happen, you will be in a much better position to handle what really *does* happen.

There are several key benefits to preparing for your interviews:

- You will put your best foot forward—no matter what happens.
- You will eliminate awkward moments and stumbling blocks.
- You will be prepared to handle (and even turn around) a bad interview. Few of the people who interview you will be professional interviewers, so you will likely get into some interviews that are hard to read and hard to handle.

Prior to the interview:

There are several things you should do, one or two days prior to the interview:

- **Know your audience**

  Find out as much as you can about the person or people you are meeting. If the meeting is by referral, circle back to the person who referred you and get as much information as you can. If you are going in cold, do an Internet search, go to your network (online networks are especially powerful for this), and see if anyone knows this person or people. You may be amazed at what you can find out.

- **Research the company.**

  Know what business they are in and read recent press releases. If you know anyone who works there (or who has worked there in the past), call them and ask for them to chat with you about the company and its culture.

- **Anticipate the questions.**

Prepare a list of questions you think you'll be asked. There are many places to find typical interview questions. You will find sample interview questions on the next page. Feel free to do more research and, certainly, ask anyone who knows anything about the hiring manager whether they know how her interviews typically go, what types of questions she asks.

Once again, keep it simple and remember that anyone interviewing you wants to know three basic things:

"Do you fit?"

> This is obvious, and yet you can easily be diverted during an interview. Also, very often what the hiring manager really wants is not clear until you are sitting in front of him (even then, it can be tough to know). You must listen carefully in the interview and ask the interviewer to clarify if you do not understand the question. Make sure you know what is important to them. Listen. Focus on what you know he wants in the candidate (based upon the job posting, prior conversations, etc.), and listen for the not-so-obvious ones. What is "the fit?" (Skills, compensation, and demonstrated success in similar roles.)

"Will you fit the team and company culture?"

> This is a question of personality and "soft skills." Be professional, be courteous, and yet make sure you are true to yourself. People like to work with people who are touchable. Do not change who you are. Either you will fit in, or you will not. Better to be yourself and find out now that this is not the place for you than to put on airs only to discover you hate the people and the culture.

"Do you want the job?"

> I have seen more spectacular candidates lose the perfect job because of this last issue than I care to remember. Why? Because people want to hire individuals who are motivated to work with them, and who are excited about the opportunity. Even if you interview well and have the perfect skills, if the hiring manager does not think you really want the job, she will go with another candidate who clearly wants the job. Why? She knows that performance on the job is directly related to your personal motivation. And if you seem ho-hum about the opportunity, chances are you will be ho-hum about the job and either not perform well or leave for another opportunity early on. Most hiring managers will hire someone with fewer skills but more passion than someone who has all the right skills and is ho-hum about the opportunity.

> **Please note:** I simply mean, "Show your enthusiasm!" I do not mean fake it. Not at all. If you get in there are you do not think this is a fit, do not jump over the moon for it. However, if you think you might be interested and want to chew on it, you must give the interviewer the impression that you are very interested. What you cannot undo is mediocre enthusiasm and a lost opportunity.

- **Develop your own questions.**

  Create a list of five to ten questions *you* would like to have answered during the interview. Don't write down the obvious. Rather, write some in-depth questions that will do two things. First, help you decide if this really is the right move for you. Second, indicate that you are serious about exploring this opportunity.

  Use **Worksheet 11: What I want** to guide the development of this list. Also, listen to your gut and concerns about this job, and build questions around that. Skip questions like, "What are your hours of operation?" Those are questions for much later in the process (unless, of course, you think this job might be graveyard shift, and you need to work days), when you are seriously considering this job. For some sample questions around key issues, go to the next page.

- **Practice.**

  Seriously. Talk to yourself. Practice with a significant other and/or your champion. Like anything in life, to be great, you must practice. Even though I know and you know you've got all the right stuff, the key is to make sure it shines through in the interview. You've spent a lot of time figuring out what makes you great, what people need to know about you. Now is the time to practice telling people those things—clearly and concisely. If you do not practice, you will be in danger of either forgetting some key things to share, or rambling on in an interview. It is especially important to practice answering the tough question.

  Refer back to the "Name your fears" exercise and practice talking quickly through the interview questions you fear the most. One of the biggest stumbling blocks for people is the simple question, "Tell me about yourself." Another tough one is, "Why did you leave that job?"

The more you practice, the luckier you'll be.
- Author Unknown

Sample interview questions

Here are some sample questions asked during job interviews:

- Tell me about yourself.
- Give me a brief review of your background.
- Why should I hire you?
- What did you like/ dislike about your former employer?
- Why did you leave that job?
- Why are you interested in our company?
- Why are you interested in this job?
- What do you want in your next job?
- What are your strengths?
- What are your weaknesses?
- What is your desired compensation?
- What other opportunities are you pursuing?
- Tell me about your proudest career moment.

- Tell me about your *least* proud career moment.
- Your background seems to be more _____ than _____. We really need someone with solid _____ skills. Help us understand (briefly) how what you've done fits this role.
- If we hired you today, how do you think you might help us?

Here are some sample questions for you to ask, on some key issues.

What you want to know:

What is your company culture?

How to ask:

- Why did you join this company?
- What do you like about working here?
- Why do you think your best employees are happy at this company, on this team, etc.?
- What type of people would you say really thrive in this environment?
- What happens when projects are in danger of running over budget or deadlines?
- How do you handle work during peak business periods? Hire contractors, work overtime, push deadlines?
- How will I know, three months from now, that I am exceeding your expectations?
- How do you like your employees to communicate with you?
- Who is your top employee, and why?

How do you evaluate success?

How to ask:

- How will you know, 6 months from now, that you made the right decision by hiring me?
- What should I accomplish in my first 6 months to become your top employee?

Am I qualified? What am I missing? What are your concerns? Will I move ahead in the process?

How to ask

- Based upon our meeting today, do you see me as a potential fit for this position?
- After meeting with me today, do you see any gaps in my experience and what you need for this position?

What are the next steps? (Timeline, what to expect)

How to ask:

- What are the next steps in your process?
- Where do we go from here?

Take care of yourself

Get a good night's sleep. Eat breakfast. Drink lots of water. Exercise. Talk to your champions. Prior to the interview, do not drink something with bubbles (it might make you burp).

Give a firm handshake

Nothing says, "I am not confident, I am not qualified, I am not sure I want to be here" like a weak handshake. Crushing a hand is no good, either.

Top tips for a great handshake:

- Let the webs of your hands touch.
- Make strong eye contact.
- Smile!

Be professional, yet touchable.

You know yourself best

How do you react under pressure, when you are meeting people for the first time? If you tend to be stiff and reserved, focus on relaxing and thinking of this interview as a social visit. Remember that the person interviewing you is human and fallible, too. If you tend to be casual and get comfortable quickly or spill your guts when you get nervous, focus on being more professional and buttoned-up than normal.

Never share personal details or get too comfortable in an interview. Never assume things are going well and you can "let it all hang out." I am amazed at the things people sometimes share with me in an interview situation. Unfortunately, once you share, those things cannot be taken back, even if you want to. Keep the conversation focused on the job at hand.

Let the interviewer drive

Something few people understand, or they forget it in an interview, is that the interviewer is in the driver's seat and he needs to be. The interviewer holds the key to what might be your dream job. He's got to get through his questions to be able to effectively compare you against other candidates. Give him what he needs. You do not want him leaving the interview with questions unanswered. You do not have to get it all done in one meeting; you will have time to get your questions answered. If you interview with a company who does not give you time to ask *your* questions, do not despair. You *will* be able to get your questions answered before you accept a job. If not, be wary of that company.

Close the deal

Now, close the deal. Ask about next steps. Share your enthusiasm for the position. It does not matter what you say, but **you must end the interview with something that**

indicates you want the job, or at least that you are interested in learning more. Passion sells!

Sample things to say:

- Well, thank you very much for your time today. Based upon what we've talked about, I am very interested in learning more. What are the next steps and where are you in your interviewing process?
- Thanks so much for your time today, (person's name). It sounds like a great opportunity. I know I could do a great job for you. What do you think?
- Do you have any concerns – anything else you'd like to know about me?
- Did I answer all of your questions today?
- I am very interested in this position. May I ask you what you think? Am I a good fit for this opportunity?

Occasionally, interviewers will be uncomfortable with a direct question about what they think about you, but that is okay. If you are enthusiastic and smile, they will walk away remembering that you are excited about working with them.

Say "Thank you"

Always say, "Thank you!" Start as you leave the meeting, and, later, send a quick email and a **handwritten** note.

Send the thank you email that day. Send a handwritten thank you note in the mail right away. No, this is not overkill. It will put you on top of the list of potential hires. Nobody sends the personal touch anymore, and this is important. So do it!

Debrief

Debrief after the interview--with yourself and with your champion(s). The only way to learn, and to effectively evaluate one opportunity against another, is to spend some time reflecting on the interview you just had. Before you get into anything else in life, go sit down in a quiet place (a coffee shop works well), be very honest, and ask yourself these questions (be very specific).

- Did the interview go well?
- If so, why?
- If not, why not?
- What excited you about the job?
- What are your concerns about the job?
- Do I have the skills they are looking for?
- If so, be specific about which ones you have and why you think you've got what it takes.
- If not, why not?
- If you are not sure, be specific about what you think based upon the interview you just had.
- What did you do well in the interview?
- What did you *not* do well in the interview?
- Were there any awkward moments?
- If so, what were they about and why were they awkward?"

- What could you have done better in the interview?
- What do you need to practice answering for the next interview?
- Are you a top candidate for this position?
- If you think so, write down why.
- If you do not think so, write down why not.
- How does this job fit what you want?

Take your answers to these questions and review them against what you want, and against your other opportunities. The more realistic you are about your chances of getting a job (or your desire to get the job), the smarter you will be with where you spend your time and how you check your emotions along the way.

Follow up

You went on an interview, and you want the job. It has been a week and you have not heard from the recruiter or the hiring manager. Should you follow up? Absolutely!

Once again, passion sells. And checking back in is a great way to say "I am really interested" as well as "I am the kind of person who will not wait around to get something resolved. I will keep checking in until I either get a status update, or know the issue is dead." This is a great way to make a positive impression.

Caution: Persistence is good, but becoming a pest is not. Some candidates do too much following up. You do not want to seem desperate, and you do not want to be a pest. Once a week is ample. More than that is bordering on too much (unless something legitimate changes on your end, such as, "I have a job offer from another company, but I am very interested in yours! Where are you in the process? How do I stand next to your other candidates? How soon can you make a decision?"

"How long should I expect to wait?"

There are so many factors affecting this, it is tough to pin down just how long the hiring process will take. The best way to know is to ask that question along the way. It is fair, appropriate, and normal to ask "What are the next steps in your process, and how long do you anticipate it will take?" Believe it or not, if you are applying for a job with the government, the whole process can take up to six months. You'll have to be patient. And keep your pipeline full of other opportunities. I watch WAY too many people say "That interview went so well, I just know I got the job. I'm just waiting to hear." Do NOT fall into this trap. You do not have the job until you have a written job offer … and even then, I have seen deals fall apart at the last minute.

Below, I outline some reasons why companies may not move as fast as you want them to:

1. **The budget has not yet been approved.** Yes, it happens all the time. A hiring manager gets verbal approval, but not formal approval. He or she knows that they need to start interviewing now, or it will take them weeks or months to hire. But you may get caught in between the verbal and formal approval.

2. **The interviewers and decision-makers are busy with many priorities.** While hiring for this position is important, there are bigger fires burning that simply get in the way.

3. **Recruiters / HR folks are buried with work**, and cannot get it all done as fast as they should. This is why the candidate who is easiest to work with, and best articulates why he is a fit for the job, gets hired. If a corporate recruiter is driving the process, they are often carrying 30-40 open positions. Think about the volume of resumes, phone screens, interviews, coordination efforts they are going through. It takes on average 10-20 hours per position to hire someone. Imagine. A 40-hour work week. 1 hour per week per position. You can see what's happening. So, when you don't get return calls, it is rarely personal.

4. **Priorities change**, and they are trying to figure out if hiring for your position is mission-critical or not.

5. **Internal candidates show up** late in the process. The company will, and should, interview those candidates.

6. **Other candidates show up** late, and they will stall you and interview them all before they make a decision. Getting all of the final candidates scheduled for interviews and through the process can sometimes take weeks.

7. **You're not dealing with the decision-maker.** I learned this the hard way when I started selling IT consulting services (essentially, I was selling contractors to companies). You can get caught up in the romance of a great relationship, thinking you're gonna win ... and fail to ask the tough questions. Often, the person who seems to be in control of the hiring decision is not. The person in charge **may be looking for something different in a new hire.** You think you've got all the right stuff, and inside, they're not talking with each other. Time and time again, I have seen the job requirements change last-minute because the people on the inside are not clearly defining the hiring criteria. Asking the question "So, what is the process for making the final decision about who to hire?" is a great one. Or, "How will you choose your final candidate?"

You cannot control any of this. However, knowledge is power. If you keep asking the right questions, and make sure you are that candidate who is easy to work with, you will be much more likely to stay on top of the pile. Or, you will be more likely to find out the bad news early on that you are not a fit. Both options beat sitting in the dark, wondering if you should put any more energy into it.

Control what you can control – and let the rest go.

How to Talk About Money

Money needs special attention for two reasons. It is very important, and it is tough to talk about. There should be no surprises once a job offer is made. Often, nobody talks about money at all during the interview process. Everyone makes assumptions and when the company puts out a job offer, you are sorely disappointed. Thus begin fruitless negotiations that leave everyone feeling undervalued.

I know that there are countless books on job hunting that tell you never to discuss salary. I disagree. Take it as you wish. I have watched many deals fall apart because neither side was forthcoming and expectations were missed. It is not funny. On the other hand, I have personally guided and watched countless situations where, if left untouched, the deal would have been broken. However, if conversations about money begin early on, either the company will decide to offer more money (this takes time to get approved and it is not easy to get approval after the offer has been made) or the candidate will reset his expectations slightly. Compensation is negotiable, but, rarely after the offer is extended.

Handle References Well

At some point in the hiring process, you will get asked for references. Here are some tips on how to manage the process of giving and nurturing your references, making sure they help you put your best foot forward.

Make a list of at least five people you feel you can ask to give you a positive reference. Then, protect that list with your life.

- Call each of your potential references ahead of time and get their permission to list them as a reference. Tell them you are on the hunt for something new and ask if they would be comfortable standing as a reference for you. Just because you *think* they will be happy to give you a reference does not mean they will. I am always astonished when I call references a candidate gives me and the reference is reluctant to talk, or actually gives a bad reference (almost every time this happens, it is because the candidate did not call to ask permission). If your reference does not feel great about you, sometimes the most damaging reference can be what they *do not say* (their tone of voice, lack of enthusiasm, etc.).

- Do not list your references on your resume. You do not want your references getting calls without your permission, and you want to be well aware when your references are getting calls.

- Do not give your list of references out at every meeting. Wait until you are asked and, even then, only if you have a real job opportunity. You do not want your references overworked by long-shot opportunities.

- When you do give out your list of references, call each of them and tell them about the position you are interviewing for, why you are interested, and find out their availability. Ask for their opinion and advice. If they care enough about you to stand as a reference, they will appreciate this phone call. It will help them put your best foot forward for the job. Let your reference into your inner circle. Let them help you overcome the potential concerns. Now this person will be a powerful reference for you.

Negotiate for What You Want

What is negotiable?

Everything. Some things. Nothing. I am afraid there is no easy answer here. The answer is unique to you, the company, and the position. However, there are steps you can (and must!) take to determine whether you can negotiate for more pay, more vacation, bigger role, later start date, or any host of other things. If you know what you want, you know you are a top contender, and it becomes much easier to ask for what you want.

When should negotiations begin?

Negotiation should begin before the job offer arrives. In fact, it is going on at each step of the interview process. It is your job to pay attention, ask questions, and understand if there are some things missing for you so you can bring it to the attention of the recruiter or hiring manager early on. Many people will argue with me on this. But, after years of watching deals fall apart after the fact, I stand firm on this. You must begin addressing your concerns, bridging the gaps, and negotiating before the final offer comes. I tell companies the same thing. You want to get it right the first time so everyone who signs up feels really good about the deal. If you have to beg for another $3,000, you will not feel good. If you have told the company all along that you will be happy at $95K and then you ask for $5K more when they make you an offer, the best case scenario is that they will give it to you, feeling bruised. The worst-case scenario is that they will not give it to you and you will both lose out.

What many candidates do not understand is that, yes, pay may be negotiable, but rarely after the job offer is made. You are not buying a car or a home. Employers do not like to negotiate after the fact, and doing so starts to eat away at your credibility. Unfortunately, some companies are bad at interviewing and they do not ask the right questions during the hiring process. That often leaves people with job offers below what they want and need. So make sure you talk about compensation before the employer puts together a job offer. You don't want to ask about compensation in the first interview, but it is absolutely appropriate to talk about it once you are a final candidate. If the person must ask for approval to pay you above budget, he will look stupid asking for it after the fact. Bad news does not get better with time. It is much easier to get approval to stretch the budget, wiggle on vacation policy or hours, if he can prepare the decision maker ahead of time.

Both parties need to feel they are getting something. Negotiation is about compromise. If you are asking for something big, be prepared to wiggle on something else you want.

Why is it taking so long? How long should I expect to wait?

There are so many factors affecting this, it is impossible to tell you how long one particular hiring process will take unless I am the recruiter working on the position. Even then, I do not always know because things change. The best way to know is to ask that question along the way. It is fair, appropriate, and normal to ask "What are the next steps in your process, and how long do you anticipate it taking?"

Here are some classic reasons why the process does not move as fast as you want it to:

- The budget for the position has not yet been formally approved, so they are moving slowly.
- There are a lot of other candidates interviewing, and they have to go through all of them, even if you are their top pick so far.
- The corporate recruiter handling the job you want has 20-40 open positions on his desk, and simply cannot get it all done as quickly as he would like.
- The decision makers are busy and not able to get together to discuss the candidates.

- The position is confidential, and so they are moving delicately through the process
- Key players are out of the office and unavailable.
- You are not their top pick so far, but they do not want to let you go because the other candidate might fall apart.

In summary, you have a lot of control during the interview process. Use **Worksheet 15: Job Hunt Scorecard** to guide you as you go. Be prepared. Ask the right questions. Be enthusiastic, and ask for the job. You will be amazed at what can happen once you start to take control of your side of the process.

Get the Job

It sounds simple and, by this stage, it should be rather simple to get the job (compared to all the heavy lifting you have done). But I need to caution you. It is not over until it is over. The job is not yours until you have it in writing, and really, until your first 90 days on a new job are up. So do not rest on your laurels just yet.

Remember: This is not about getting just any job. This is about getting a job you will love. So first, you need to keep your eye on the ball and make sure you get the offer you want. Second, you need to make sure it is real before you quit your job hunt, or quit your current job.

There are a few things to keep in mind as you negotiate this final stage of the job interviewing process.

Choose the job that's right for you

You've come this far; do not lose sight of what you want! Whether you have one job offer or three to consider, you must choose the job that is right for you—today and tomorrow. Do not jump at the first job to come along, and hope it works out. Ask the questions. Trust your gut. Talk to your champions.

Catherine's story:

> "I can tell you from personal experience that there is nothing worse than landing in a job you hate and then realizing that you would have known better if you simply asked the right questions. I should have been in control of my job hunt, but I was not. I was anxious to get a job, I liked the people and I was intrigued by the business. I thought it would be a great way to expand my skills. It would have been, if I could have tolerated the company culture. I failed to ask the tough (but critical) questions during the interview process. That was my experience, and it was a really painful one. Because I made that mistake, I ended up out on the job market again, looking for a new job three months later. Not fun. Had I walked away during the interview process, I would have landed my dream job the first time around, for more money!"

How to choose the job that's right for you:

- Trust your gut. If your little voice is yelling at you, or even talking softly in your ear, you need to listen! Ninety nine percent of the time when I ask people, "Did you know in your gut, when you accepted the job, that it was not the right one for you?" they will admit, "Yes, I did."
- Use your list of "non-negotiables."
- Use your list of "what I want."
- Use the job attribute scorecard.
- Use your trusted advisors (champions) as a sounding board.
- Sleep on it.
- Ask for one more conversation with the hiring manager if you have small reservations or questions that are nagging you.

Caution at the finish line

Remember: *A job is not yours until you have it in writing, so you must keep up your job hunt efforts full steam away until you have a written job offer!*

Do not say yes, or quit your current job, until you have your job offer in writing.

You may accept an offer verbally, but let the hiring manager know it is an informal acceptance until you get an offer letter. You must see everything in writing—Job title, duties, compensation, and benefits. For instance, does your healthcare kick in right away, or do you have to wait 6 months? What about your 401K? When can you start contributing to that? What about bonuses, 30-day expectations and start date? Many people accept jobs where the employer says, "We'll work that out with you once you start." I am here to tell you that no, they will not. You are never more powerful than when a job offer has been extended and the company is waiting for you to start. If you have a bonus plan, insist on getting it in writing. If you are going to work for a small company that has never written a formal offer letter, be concerned. And then be helpful. Find a sample on the Internet and create it based upon what you understand the job to be. A formal job offer is an agreement to terms. If asking for a formal letter means you lose the job, you do not want to work for that company. If they do not care enough about you now, they will care less about you once you are on board.

Do not quit your current job until you have everything in writing, including a start date.

A special note for people considering bonus and/or commissions: Do not accept a job until you see your commission plan and/or bonus plan in writing, it has been explained to you, and you are crystal clear about what you need to do to get paid. You will have no right to dispute a bonus you were told verbally would be 10% unless you have it in writing. I won't go into details of the many sad people I have seen do this on faith. Do not do it! If the company is not serious enough about you to take the time to write it down and explain it to you, that company is not serious about you succeeding, nor are they serious about paying you that bonus they boasted about in the hiring process to entice you to join.

Why, am I so adamant about this? Because I see it happen all the time, with best intentions. Job offers are extended. Then, hiring managers go away, budgets get dropped, people quit or get fired, mergers and acquisitions put all hiring on hold. And there you will stand, holding the bag and unable to get what was promised you. You must protect yourself against these unforeseen circumstances. A formal offer letter is not a guarantee your job won't go away, but it is a much better assurance than anything else.

Quit your job the right way

"How you leave is how you enter."
— Author unknown

I know it's tempting to tell your boss everything that has been wrong with his or her methods for the last year. Do not do it. It will haunt you. No matter how right you are or how wronged you have been, you will be the one left looking bad if you exit unprofessionally. What is there to gain besides a few minutes of glory? Nothing. So exit gracefully, protect your reputation, and be relieved that you are moving on to something new and wonderful.

The correct steps to take, no matter what the situation, are as follows:

- **Write a formal resignation letter.**

- **Give a minimum or two weeks' notice, a maximum of three weeks' notice.** A word of caution to you loyal employees. If your current employer asks you to give four weeks' notice, I strongly urge you not to. I watch this happen all the time. The first two weeks are fine. The third week is tough. But the fourth week is simply painful—for everyone. It is like a long, drawn-out breakup and it simply gets ugly. It is far too long for people to say goodbye, and it will be far too long for you. I have watched great people with great intentions try to do the right thing by giving four weeks, and it is simply too much.

- **Quit with your boss before you tell your colleagues**, even if your boss is a jerk.

- **Be professional and positive.** I know you do not feel like being positive on your way out the door, but this is a small world. You will undoubtedly bump into your colleagues down the road. You need them to speak well of you. There is no value in being negative or running down a list of all he reasons you hate working at this current employer. Do that with your champion, where you know it will not come back to haunt you.

- **Sketch out a transition plan to review with your supervisor when you quit.** If you go to your boss with a very high-level list of what you feel needs to be transitioned and suggestions for how to do that (including, if you'd like, who you think would handle something well), he or she will not be nearly as panicked about losing you, *and* will see that you have full intentions of leaving them in good shape.

- **Practice your resignation speech.** Short, sweet, and to the point.

- **Review your reasons for taking the new job** as you prepare for this. Make sure you are certain, in your heart, that this is the right move for you. And then, repeat it to yourself over and over.

- **Be ready for the counter offer and guilt trip—whatever comes your way.** And practice handling it. What are you going to say if your boss says, "I am grooming you for the Director role. Who am I going to put in your place? How am I going to replace you? I do not know what we are going to do without you," etc. etc. etc. Do not even engage in this conversation and ask questions like, "Why am I only hearing this now?" You know why, and those reasons will not change (if this is the case).

- **Stay in solution mode (smooth transition mode).** If your boss pushes you for more than three weeks' notice, or says "We cannot make it without you," then move into solution mode. Ask about his concerns, what he thinks you can do in that fourth week that you cannot accomplish in three weeks. Ensure him that while you will not be there to get _____ project out the door, you will take great pains to make this a smooth transition.

Remember: *There is no shame. There is no guilt. This is exciting and you are taking an important and exciting new step for your own personal growth and satisfaction. The company takes care of itself first, and you must take care of yourself first. Your manager will understand that, once the initial shock passes.*

In summary, you have worked this hard and come this far. Take this one last step to leave gracefully. Your reputation is at stake, and it is worth protecting.

Expect a counter offer

If you are gainfully employed and in good standing with your current employer, be prepared to receive a counter offer. A "counter offer" is simply an employer's offer to entice you to stay on once you have given them your resignation latter. This offer often comes with attractive options (usually those you were not getting from them until now, which prompted you to look elsewhere in the first place).

There is a dangerous allure in a counter offer. I spoke about this briefly early on when I asked you, "Can you stay where you are to get what you want?" Answer this question **before you quit!** You must make an objective, rational decision about this before your emotions get tied up with the people at your current job. You must be very clear about why you are leaving, and hold that close to your heart as you face the difficult prospect of a counter offer.

To quit or not to quit is often a gut-wrenching decision. It is a major life decision that requires abandoning the comfort of the old and welcoming the risk of the new. There is the people side. You undoubtedly work with people you like and care about. You might be leaving them with your workload for temporarily. There is also the danger of making the wrong decision. So, weigh your decision carefully, **before you quit**, because accepting a counter offer is almost never a good idea.

A counter offer usually comes through with one of the following:

- More money
- More flexibility
- A promotion, or the promise of one
- Promises to give you the job you want
- Disparaging remarks about the new employer
- Guilt trips like, "We really need you. You are so important to our team, we cannot do it without you. Please reconsider."

So often, people take a new job and quit without asking for what they want or anticipating a counter offer. Then, on the day they quit, their boss says "Gee, why didn't you ask me?"

Max's story:

Max sat down to tell his boss he was quitting.

Boss: "Max, why are you leaving?"

Max: "Well, I wanted more responsibility and more money. I was waiting for a promotion and it never came."

Boss: "Well, Max, we can give you what you want. In fact, I was just about to promote you and give you a pay raise. I have the approval paperwork sitting on my desk. Susan is out of town, so I cannot get her signature until Friday, but I was excited about moving you into this new role. We would really hate to lose you. How can I get you to stay?"

So what's the problem? Max can take the promotion and stay. Right? Not so fast. First, he has to ask himself why the promotion did not come sooner, why he had no idea it was coming, and if the culture is really the reason he wanted to leave in the first place (not lack of promotion or raise). There are probably some communication issues that will not change even if he stays. Also, if it takes the threat of quitting to get the raise that he wanted, he needs to ask the question "Why?" and consider that perhaps he is not valued the way he would like to be.

The second reason Max should think long and hard about this is this: once the cat is out of the bag that he's looked outside, there is no getting it back in. Will they hold it against Max? Will they pass him over for future promotions and opportunities because he has had one foot out the door? It's a question which, unaddressed, has some serious ramifications. However, only Max can answer this, and navigate this. Contrary to popular opinion, you should be very careful before using a job offer to negotiate for what you want at your current employer should be a last resort.

Smart companies rarely make counter offers, because they know it is too late, that you have one foot out the door, and that they need to let you go graciously. However, many companies find themselves scared to lose you, and will do anything they can to hold onto you until they can get through a critical phase, and/or hire a replacement for you. Your boss may be genuine about wanting you to stay, but you cannot undo the damage once you resign. The cat is out of the bag. They know your heart is not where it once was for the company.

In summary, you need to expect a counter offer and be prepared to say "No." If you are not prepared to say "No," you need to question whether or not you should be quitting. Perhaps you really want to stay and make the job you have a better one.

STEP 4: Keep It!

Hooray! Warmest congratulations on your new job. It is simply fantastic that you are here now, and you must stop to pat yourself on the back. Yes, you got some help along the way, but you—and only you—are responsible for getting this job. So rejoice and be proud of your hard work. Enjoy the next few days or weeks before you start your new adventure, and take it easy on yourself.

There are some things you need to do to wrap up your job hunt, and also some things you need to do moving forward to help you succeed on this new job, and also in the rest of your career. Let's run through these things quickly for you.

Go Yell it From the Mountain! (Take 2)

This is such exciting news, you really must share it!

Let your intimate network know that you have found and accepted a job.

Go call them and then come back! This is much too great to keep to yourself.

Wasn't that fun?

Let your broader network know via email

Yes, every single person you spoke to during your search should hear the wonderful news. Send a short note to your entire network, letting them know that you have landed somewhere new and thanking them all for their assistance! It would be great to send another email out to your network once you start at your new employer (maybe one or two weeks in) and give them your new work contact information.

Here are some sample emails announcing the fabulous news.

- **Email subject line:** Accepted a position with ABC Corp.

  Hello! I have landed in a great new job as _____ at _____.
  Thank you for all of your help during the past months with my job search. I could not have done it without you all. Your tips and referrals were a great help. I believe ABC Corp. will be a great fit for me and for them. Thanks again! Please let's make a point of staying in touch, and let me know if and when I can help you in any way.

  Best regards,

  John

- **Email subject line:** I landed!

Just wanted to let you all know that I have accepted a new position with XYZ Inc. and will be starting with them on October 3rd as their finance administrator. My job hunt has actually been a wonderful process, learning about so many people and companies. I am confident that XYZ will be a great place for me, and that I will add a lot of value there as well. So many thanks are in order, I will be reaching out to you in person, but I wanted to share the great news immediately. I will stay in touch, and look forward to assisting you in your career whenever you call.

Cheers!

Connie

Thank Everyone Who Helped You During Your Search

Do something nice for those few who really hung in there with you.

Your champions were there for you throughout your job hunt and it is time to thank them for their time and commitment. You know who they are. Your gift does not have to be expensive, but it should be thoughtful. If you are short on cash, cook a nice dinner (why not invite them all at the same time to help you celebrate?) or give a handwritten card, along with home-baked cookies. You really should do something extra special for them. It is not the price that matters. It is the recognition and the thoughtfulness.

Launch for Success

The first 90 days are the most important days of your new career with this employer. It will set the stage for your success or failure with this company. Recovering from a rough first 90 days is difficult. On the other hand, if you start off with gusto and really pay attention to what you are delivering, how you are meeting expectations, it will pay off tenfold. You will be seen, from the beginning, as someone to pay attention to, someone to groom for bigger things, someone to help get to the next level.

Sadly, few companies do a good job of launching their new employees. Honestly, the first few weeks are usually a wash if the new employer is unprepared for new hires. Do not sit and wait for them to come with you. Take the initiative. If you are sitting there twiddling your thumbs, do something about it. Talk to your new boss. Talk to your new colleagues and ask what you can help them with. Do not sit idle and be happy with mediocrity. Make a difference.

Here are some tips on how to make your first 90 days really great, and set the stage for a long and happy career at your new company.

Deliver results quickly

Get a clear understanding of the urgent needs or priorities you are expected to deliver right away and dig right in.

- Ask for a 30-day review with your new boss. Make it a one-on-one meeting (preferably out of the office, over coffee or lunch, alone). Offer to buy lunch. Make sure you are delivering above expectations, and if you are not, find out why. Do not be afraid to ask the difficult questions. People know that you are new and learning, and they will be very forgiving in the first 90 days, so leverage that time to find out exactly what you are doing well and where you need improvement. Then fix it.

- Ask for a 60-day review with your new boss and repeat above.

- Ask for a 90-day review with your new boss, and any other key players, and repeat above.

Get to know people

- Come up with two or three questions you are comfortable asking people when you meet them for the first time.

  For example, "How did you come to work here?" "How long have you been here?" "What are you working on right now?" Another good question (depending on the audience) is, "What is one thing you suggest I do to ramp up quickly?" Or ask a fun one question like, "What was your first job ever?"

- Ask people to grab lunch with you.
- Be courteous.
- Do not be a pest.

You do not want to make a pest of yourself, and people are busy. Some questions can wait. When I start new employees, I always set a standing meeting with them (daily during the first week, every two or three days after that for the first month). This meeting does not have to be in person, and it can be very quick. I suggest that you keep a list of questions you add to throughout the day. If they are urgent, of course, you need to ask them right away. But most of your questions can wait.

Pay it Forward

Help people network

You need to take the time (even if it is only five or ten minutes on the phone) to help someone's network keep moving.

Help vendors /sales people

What do you do about all those sales people who call on you because they want you to buy from them? Be nice to them, and consider helping them to be successful in their business, too. The thing is, vendors have a view on your industry, your competition and even your business that you do not have, sitting on the inside. If you like them and trust them, build a trusted relationship that will serve you both well for years to come. Trust your instincts; if you do not trust the integrity of a vendor, then go find another one.

If you treat your vendors well, they will be there for you when you are looking to take your business to the next level, and also when you are looking for a new job.   So be nice. . I go out of my way to help clients and vendors who have been great to work with … whether or not it will serve my business today. I also think twice before exposing my network to the handful of clients and vendors who have not been professional … because my network trusts me to treat people with dignity and respect.

Everyone matters!

If you are not helpful to someone today, they will remember it down the road when you need it—and they will not help you. I see it every day! I'd like you to be good to others just because it is the right thing to do. Sometimes, work and life get in the way and people think "I want to—but don't have time right now."

Here is a painful lesson learned by one job seeker:

> Early in his career, he did not network well. He did not help people when they asked for it (in fact, he turned me down when I asked him for help a few years ago). He was a friend of a friend … I'd even been camping with his family). He did not understand what networking is all about and found it safer to stay in his job and say no instead of reaching out, meeting and helping people. This behavior really hurt him last year when he was laid off and out on the hunt for a new job. Despite the fact that he had been quite rude when I called to ask for help a few years ago, I did try to help him network (he is, after all, a friend of a friend). I asked one person in my network to help him, and guess what his response was? "No way. I am not helping him. I asked him for help awhile back and he said no." He learned his lesson, the hard way. This is what he said to me, once he finally landed in a great new job:

> "I do solemnly swear that I will faithfully execute my limited networking skills and connections to help professionals who are in need of a stripe change or other professional assistance when called upon while I am in or out of the office of my next position, providing my next position is confirmed to be a position where I will work without fear and micro pressure from five foot tall or so command and control supervision freaks. I will do so to the best of my ability, in an effort to help stripe changing professionals achieve a productive and happy place (within reason) in order to become stronger contributors to society and help their well being (again, within reason and in a non-gluttonous fashion). Viva la the professional network!"

See? We can all change our stripes. So let go of whatever has gone before, and strike a new path for yourself.

Keep Your Network Alive

Keeping your network alive is quite simple, and you now understand why this is so important. You do not want to start networking from scratch the next time you need a new job. But you must make it a priority and set some goals around it.

Here are some suggestions:

- Attend at least one new networking event per month.
- Commit to at least one networking group that you will attend on a very regular basis.
- Have at least one networking meeting per month (coffee, lunch, drinks).
- Keep your online social networking presence alive and updated.
- Find somewhere to contribute as a guest speaker, article contributor, or volunteer.

Keep Dreaming!

It is simply terrific that you have landed a great new job. Go knock their socks off! But keep your network, and your search for work that you love, alive.

Change is inevitable. Companies get sold, great bosses leave and rotten bosses arrive, people get laid off. Your personal life changes as well. Your needs change, and what you want today is not what you will want five years from now. Even if you just landed your dream job today, it will change and you will change at some point. To do what you love for a living, you must see this as a lifelong process. Change is the one thing you can count on in your career. I can almost guarantee you that this will not be your last job or your last company in your career. Gone are the days when people sit inside one company for 25 years. And that is not necessarily a bad thing. In fact, I think it is great, because people have much greater potential to chase their dreams and do what they love for a living. But you must stay in the driver's seat. Now that you have gone through this "*Change Your Stripes*" process, you know what you need to do to stay on top of your career and your future happiness. Make it a commitment to stay connected, keep your resume updated, and keep chasing those dreams. Your dreams might change, but the ability for you to go get them will not. You are in control of your destiny. Do you want to sit back and wait for the next shoe to drop, or do you want to go grab the life you want?

Here are some suggestions for you to stay ahead of, and in control of, career change and happiness:

- Stay connected and up to date on the latest in job hunting information on the www.arbez.com web site.

- Update your "what I want" and "what I do not want" list annually, or more often if you sense change on the horizon.

- Keep notes on every great thing you do at work, to help build future resumes and capture what makes you great. Be sure to capture data (such as return on investment, cost savings, increased revenue, what your benefit was to the company, etc.).

- Stay connected—online through social and professional networking sites and in person through regular coffee or lunch meetings.

- Build your own "board of advisors." Select a handful of people you consider your mentors, excellent connections in your life, and make regular connections with them. Stay on top of their career, as well as yours.

- Find someone to mentor. We often learn and grow the most through helping other people. It will keep you sharp and keep you connected.

- Sharpen your saw regularly. Make sure you are getting ongoing training, refreshing your technical, business and networking skills. Do not stagnate.

- Watch the market. Watch your industry. Make it a commitment to be well-read in your area of expertise.

- Have fun! If you stop having fun, that is a sure sign it is time for a change. Either fix it, or get out and into something new.

Now, go Change Your Stripes

and Do What You Love for a Living!

The Worksheets

It is one thing to think about doing something. It is another thing entirely to commit it to paper. Studies have shown that once you write down a goal, you are 8 times more likely to achieve it! Congratulations on taking this next important step, and committing what you want (and how you are going to go get) it to paper. With these worksheets, you will take control of your job hunt.

With practical exercises and templates to guide you, you will clearly define what you want in your next job, identify your target market, create a resume and cover letter that will work, and take other key steps in your job search.

You are unique, and these worksheets will help you bring your distinct talents, desires and needs to life. You will be amazed how much more powerful and directed you feel once you have worked through these simple exercises. Once you have completed these worksheets, you will have a very clear picture of what you want - and how to go get it.

Clearly, you are here because you want to find a job faster, and you want a job that is right for you. These worksheets will help you achieve both goals simultaneously. The biggest benefit to you will come from doing all the worksheets, in the right order. So, go have fun capturing what makes you great, and what you really want out of your next career move.

How to use these worksheets

I'd like to give you some tips on how to use these worksheets. My recommendation is this: start with **Worksheet 01: Protect yourself** and move on in order. I know you are anxious to get going. I know your resume is weighing heavily on your mind. I also know that starting a job search by writing a resume is like jumping into the deep end of a pool and saying "I want to learn to swim." Sure, you'll learn, but do you really want to work that hard? I promise you this: if you take a little bit of extra time up front, the hard stuff (like writing a resume) will be *much* easier. I wrote this book and built these worksheets because I was tired of seeing good people struggle to find a new job. So often, the reason is a simple one: they did not stop to ask themselves "what job do I want?" Don't work harder than you have to. Use the process. Trust the process. Do the worksheets even if you are not sure they are worth your time.

If you are one of the lucky few who already has some of the pieces put together (like, you already know what you want and who your target market is), then fantastic! You can check those off and move to the next section. Just make sure you do not jump in at the middle. The real value of this book and workbook is in the process - taking the right steps in the right order.

Your Daily Motivation:

The Key to Success is to Start

Taking a new step, uttering a new word,
is what people fear the most.
If you wait to overcome all your possible objections,
nothing will ever be attempted.

The great thing is to start.
To see an opportunity, and to pursue it,
even though in the beginning,
you're not totally sure of all the answers to your questions.

If you want to be successful you can start anytime.
Your only true failure lies in the failure to start.
The reason why so little is ever done
Is generally because so little is attempted.
If you can get up the courage to begin,
You have the courage to succeed.

(Author unknown)

Worksheet 01: Protect yourself

Finances - Action Items (What action do you need to take to protect your finances?):

Insurance - Action Items (What action do you need to take to protect your insurance needs? Consider healthcare, life insurance, short and long-term disability.)

Identify available resources - Action Items

Examples: Severance / outplacement services, unemployment insurance, workforce centers

Worksheet 02: Find a champion

There is no good reason to do this alone- and you don't have to. You will get tremendous insight and support from people if you simply ask. Think about the people in your life who will stand by your side and offer support and encouragement to you through thick and thin. It might be your spouse, your neighbor, or a colleague or two. Now write down the names of the people you think you can lean on right now. Once you have listed a few people who you know will be there for you, you need to go ask them directly for assistance during your job search. What they bring to the table will vary, but their help will be invaluable.

My Champions:

STEP 1: Know what you want

Do you know what you want next in your career? If you do, that is terrific. Jump ahead to Worksheet 10: My non-negotiables. But you might want to skim through these worksheets along the way. You might be surprised by what you discover.

If you are like most people, you probably are not very clear about what you want, and you struggle to tell other people what you want. These next worksheets will help you cut through the clutter and restrictions (real or perceived) in your life. Think boldly, and be open to new possibilities. For instance, this is not the time to say "I cannot be a _____ because I do not have any experience in _____."
Instead, this is a time to say "Boy, if I won the lottery tomorrow, I would really love to _____." You might just find that your dream job, or something close to it, is not so far out of reach for you. Reality may require you take a less-than-ideal job right now, but you can still target a better job for yourself today. You are already doing the work. It will cost you nothing more to focus on what *you* want and who *you* are while you are at it. What you stand to gain is immeasurable.

Worksheet 03: When I was a kid...

Children know how to dream shamelessly. They know exactly what they do and do not like doing, and are not afraid to say it. A great way to get in touch with your grown-up dreams is to remember what you dreamed about becoming when you were little. Chances are good that the same little voice is still inside you. Your interests have matured and shifted here and there, but often that little mini-you is more in touch with the grown-up you than you are.

I wanted to be a:

Why?

I wanted to be a:

Why?

Worksheet 04: Other people thought I would become ...

It might be fun and helpful to ask your parents, siblings or others who knew you well as a child what they thought you would become. There were undoubtedly traits they saw in you then that still live within you today.

Other people thought I would grow up to be a:

Why?

Other people thought I would grow up to be a:

Why?

They thought I would grow up to be a:

Why?

Worksheet 05: Did you chase your dreams?

Now take these lists and ask yourself "Did I chase my dreams? Has my career so far given me anything that I wanted when I was a kid?" You might be surprised to learn that yes, in fact, you are not as far away from your heart and soul as you thought you were. Our personality is a powerful driver throughout our life. There are countless small decisions we make that take us down one path versus another. Most of you will realize that your dreams are actually not that far out of reach. With just a slight shift in your job, or a new industry, you might find exactly what you want in your job.

Did you become what you wanted to become? If not, why not:

Are you still attracted to these same things? Would you still like to pursue a career in those areas?

Worksheet 06: My passion in life

Where is your passion in life? A great job is one that plays to your unique passions and your strengths. If you don't call attention to those passions, nobody else will. What do *you* love doing? Solving problems? Helping others? Empowering others? Putting the pieces together? Dig deep, and then keep digging. Once you complete this list, keep it close as you start to look at what's next in your career.

I am passionate about:

Worksheet 07: My favorite job as a teenager

You can learn a lot about yourself by taking a closer look at past jobs. I always ask people I am interviewing to tell me what they liked and disliked about previous jobs. I do that because I learn a lot about the person that way, and whether or not they will be happy in the job at hand. You may be surprised what you learn.

The job:

The job details:

Why did you like it so much?

If there was one thing you could have changed, what would that be?

Worksheet 08: My favorite job as an adult

The job:

The job details:

Why did you like it so much?

If there was one thing you could have changed, what would that be?

Worksheet 09: The job I hated most as an adult

I often hear people having "a-hah!' moments with this worksheet. For instance, you may have thought it was your boss that drove you out of your last job, but discover that it was actually the data entry and commute that drove you to leave.

The job:

The job details:

Why did you hate it so much?

What did you like about this job?

Worksheet 10: My non-negotiables

Nothing will ruin a perfectly good job faster than compromising on your core values, likes and dislikes. This is an extremely personal thing, so be sure to create this list by yourself, without input from a helpful spouse or friend. Think beyond the obvious (leadership, money) and dig into the day to day aspects of a job (commute, tools, tasks, culture, and people).

I will not:

Worksheet 11: What I want

Hooray! Now it is time to start talking about what you really want next in your career. I know you need a job right now. I know you feel you cannot be thinking about what you want, because you just need a job. I must tell you again: the candidates who know clearly what they want (even if it is as simple as commute and chance to learn) jump to the top of the candidate pile every time. Be open. Dream big. We will do a reality check shortly, which will help you identify which of your "wants" you can get right now, and which ones might have to wait.

I want:

Worksheet 12: My perfect job

Is there such a thing as a "perfect job?" Perhaps not, but wouldn't it be great to get close to your perfect job? Knowing what that would be for you will help you focus your search in the right direction, ask the right questions, and pick a job that's right for you.

Job Title:

Company:

Location:

Role:

Team:

Salary & benefits:

Day to day responsibilities:

Worksheet 13: Identify the gaps

Do you have the skills to get the job you want? Is it worth your time to even apply for the job you see? Find out by using this worksheet as a tool every time you look at an open job. Helpful hint: Tell a story for each skill you can demonstrate, using this method: STAR (S=Situation, T=Task, A=Action, R=Result). Clean, concise, effective. Not only will this help you position yourself at every step of your job search (networking, writing an effective resume, tailoring cover letters and introductions), it will also help you prepare to knock their socks off in an interview.

What is the required skill, experience or personal attribute?	Do you have the skills? Yes / No	If **yes**, write down the skill, experience or personal attribute you already have. If **not**, write down any comparable skills/experience you have. If you have nothing comparable, write down how you can get it.

What is the required skill, experience or personal attribute?	Do you have the skills? Yes / No	If **yes**, write down the skill, experience or personal attribute you already have. If **not**, write down any comparable skills/experience you have. If you have nothing comparable, write down how you can get it.

Worksheet 14: Name your fears

That thing that is scaring you is standing in the way of you getting a new job! So stop letting it control you. It doesn't have to. I promise you that every obstacle *can* be overcome. If you name them and practice handling these obstacles before they become an issue, you will move through them quickly. However, if you close your eyes and hope for the best, they will become a real barrier to getting that job you want and need.

I am afraid of ….

I will overcome this fear by….

I am afraid of ….

I will overcome this fear by….

I am afraid of ….

I will overcome this fear by….

I am afraid of ….

I will overcome this fear by….

Worksheet 15: The Job Hunt Scorecard™

Choose a job that's right for you with the Job Hunt Scorecard™

Job-hunting is a bit like planning a vacation: you do not buy plane tickets and book a trip without doing some research, and asking yourself "Will I like that place? Do I like the snow? Do I like the sea? Do I like museums?" You look at different places, compare what they offer against what you like to do. Just because your neighbor loved her trip to San Francisco does not mean that you will. A bad vacation is disappointing. A bad job can be devastating. You have the power to avoid taking a bad job! This Job Hunt Scorecard™ will help you do exactly that.

Making an objective decision about a job can be difficult, especially if you are excited about it. Emotions run high, and the stakes are high. Very often, unless you ask the right questions, you will not get the information you need to choose a job that's right for you. I see people who get very excited about a job, and avoid asking the tough questions. Then they wake up 6 months later, really unhappy and not sure why.

I know why they wake up unhappy: they did not take an objective look at the job against what they want. Just because you love the people and the mission of the company does not mean it is the right job for you. What if those people quit? What if you do not have the tools to get your job done? What if your commute is killing you? What if you accepted less money than you felt you were worth? You'll suddenly realize that people and company mission do not look so good anymore.

Use this scorecard to step away from the romance and into reality. Will this job be a good long-term fit for you? Just because your best friend loves working there does not mean you will.

HOW TO USE THE JOB HUNT SCORECARD™

FIRST, use your "What I want" and "What I don't want" worksheets as your guide to determine the 10 most important attributes of a job for you. Put your most important ones at the top and list in descending order. Notice that each thing you want is ranked. This ranking will give you a score that will help you compare one job against another, and answer the very important question "Will I be happy in this job? Will it give me what I want?" The job attribute at the top of your list should be your most important, because it is valued with a weight of ten.

NEXT, ask yourself "Will I get this in this job I am considering?" if you are not sure, you need to start asking the right questions of the employer to get answers to these questions. Circle "yes" or "no" for each.

LASTLY, give a score to each yes, and each no. You will see that the top attribute gets a score of either 10 (yes) or -10(no). The next one gets either a 9 or a -9. If you are employed right now, filled out the first column with your current job. You will now have an objective, numeric way to evaluate job opportunities.

Use this throughout your job hunt to ask the right questions. Before you go into an interview, use this scorecard as a guide, to build questions you want to get answered about the company. As you leave an interview, sit down with this to evaluate whether or not you will get what you want. And certainly, before you accept a job, run through this scorecard again and be very honest with yourself. You may end up ranking things differently. You may discover that compensation is actually 3rd on your list, not first (I can tell you that the right place for the money is usually 3rd of 4th. People rarely leave a job because of money. There are usually other "happiness factors" that trump the money one).

Tony's story:

Tony has been in product sales for ten years, and really enjoys it . His company is moving headquarters to another state and he does not want to move. He wants to find a growing company that will give him the opportunity to advance either into management or a national sales role. Most important to Tony are these three things: personal learning, career advancement and the ability to earn more than he is earning today. Next, he wants to be in a collaborative environment where he is more than just a number, where he can actually contribute beyond just the numbers. He has been commuting 2 hours a day and wants less time on the road. He has small children and having some flexibility around them is important to him. His current company is moving headquarters because they just had a hostile takeover; he wants to try to avoid a volatile situation like that again. His current company is constantly changing direction and it is difficult for him to be credible with his clients. He wants a clear strategic vision he can embrace and take to the streets. His new boss has been requiring 3 times the amount of paperwork his previous boss did, and it is getting in the way of his ability to sell, not to mention he is at his best with a desk and a phone and numbers to hit. He will raise his hand when he needs help, and wants a boss who trusts him to do that. Due to the hostile takeover, all administrative support was cut. He wants to make sure he joins a company that understands the value of sales support so that he can be out selling more.

Ranking	What I want in my next job	Present in current job?	Perceived in potential job #1?	Perceived in potential job #2?
10	Personal growth: I will be able to learn new things in this new job	No - 10	Yes + 10	Yes –+10
9	Career growth: I will be able to move up in the company. I can see that this company promotes from within.	No - 9	Yes + 9	Yes + 9
8	Money: I will make at least $_____ per year.	No - 8	No – 8	No – 8
7	Culture: I will be working in a collaborative environment, on a team, not fighting against others to get things done	Yes + 7	Yes + 7	No – 7
6	Work/life balance: Commute of no more than 45 minutes one way	Yes + 6	No – 6	No – 6
5	Work/life balance: Flexibility (ability to work from home sometimes, stay home with sick children without guilt)	Yes + 5	No – 5	No – 5
4	Solid Company: I have confidence that the company will grow and remain competitive.		No – 4	
3	Leadership: I can see a clear strategic vision that is communicated openly throughout the company	No - 3	No – 3	Yes + 3
2	Management: Hands-off: I will be trusted to get things done and raise my hand when I need help.	No - 2	Yes + 2	Yes + 2
1	Tools/resources: I can see a commitment to investing in the tools and resources I will need to be successful.	Yes + 1	Yes + 1	No – 1
Total score:		19	29	24
		-32		
		-13	+3	-3
			26	
				-27

Ranking	What I want in my next job	Present in current job?		Perceived in potential job #1?		Perceived in potential job #2?	
10		Yes +10	No – 10	Yes +10	No – 10	Yes +10	No – 10
9		Yes + 9	No – 9	Yes + 9	No – 9	Yes + 9	No – 9
8		Yes + 8	No – 8	Yes + 8	No – 8	Yes + 8	No – 8
7		Yes + 7	No – 7	Yes + 7	No – 7	Yes + 7	No – 7
6		Yes + 6	No – 6	Yes + 6	No – 6	Yes + 6	No – 6
5		Yes + 5	No – 5	Yes + 5	No – 5	Yes + 5	No – 5
4		Yes + 4	No – 4	Yes + 4	No – 4	Yes + 4	No – 4
3		Yes + 3	No – 3	Yes + 3	No – 3	Yes + 3	No – 3
2		Yes + 2	No – 2	Yes + 2	No – 2	Yes + 2	No – 2
1		Yes + 1	No - 1	Yes + 1	No - 1	Yes + 1	No – 1

Total score:

STEP 2: Know how to get it

Worksheet 16: Target job titles or roles

You are well on your way, and ready to identify your target market. Before you can craft your message effectively (tell your story, rewrite your resume), you need to know who your audience is. That will help you build a message that will work. Building your "target market" means identifying:

- Target job titles or roles
- Target industries & companies
- Target networking contacts
- Target groups and associations

On this worksheet, identify the job titles and roles that you would like to consider.

Job titles:

Worksheet 17: Target industries and companies

First, write down an industry that you know you would enjoy (because you have worked in it), as well as ones that interest you. Next, within each of those industry categories, list up to 5 companies that are of interest to you. You will very likely entertain opportunities outside of these industries and companies, but this list will help you hone your search (work smart), and help your network go to work for you as well.

Industry:

Companies:

Industry:

Companies:

Industry:

Companies:

Worksheet 18: Networking contacts

Contact information (Name, Phone Number, Email address, & contact date):

Worksheet 19: Groups and associations

Group contact information (Name, Phone Number, Email address, & contact date):

Worksheet 20: Proudest career accomplishments

Yes, you have some wonderful accomplishments to share! Highlight how your accomplishments stood out against others. Be very specific about *your* contribution, not the *team's* contribution.

Accomplishment #1

What was your job or role?

What was the SITUATION/TASK/BUSINESS PROBLEM?

What were the biggest BARRIERS or CHALLENGES?

What ACTION did you take?

What were the RESULTS?

Accomplishment #2

What was your job or role?

What was the SITUATION/TASK/BUSINESS PROBLEM?

What were the biggest BARRIERS or CHALLENGES?

What ACTION did you take?

What were the RESULTS?

Accomplishment #3

What was your job or role?

What was the SITUATION/TASK/BUSINESS PROBLEM?

What were the biggest BARRIERS or CHALLENGES?

What ACTION did you take?

What were the RESULTS?

Worksheet 21: My least proud career moment

What are those moments in *your* career you wish you could do over again? We all make mistakes. However, few of us are good at talking about those mistakes. Now is your chance to practice.

Mistake #1

What was your job or role?

What was the mistake?

Did you acknowledge it at the time or try to hide it?

Did you try to fix it and did you succeed?

What did you learn from this and what would you do differently next time?

Mistake #2

What was your job or role?

What was the mistake?

Did you acknowledge it at the time or try to hide it?

Did you try to fix it and did you succeed?

What did you learn from this and what would you do differently next time?

Mistake #3

What was your job or role?

What was the mistake?

Did you acknowledge it at the time or try to hide it?

Did you try to fix it and did you succeed?

What did you learn from this and what would you do differently next time?

Worksheet 22: My personal strengths

Do you know your strengths? We all have them. Some people are more aware of them than others. In fact, many people spend so much time trying to fix or compensate for their weaknesses that they forget to pay attention to what comes naturally. Take some time to think about where your strengths are. If you need some suggestions on these, refer back to the book, or turn to resources on discovering your strengths. These are often referred to as "soft skills," and you want to choose a job that will leverage these soft skills.

Personal strengths:

Worksheet 23: My personal weaknesses

You need to think about your weaknesses for two good reasons: first, you will get asked about them in interviews, and you want to be prepared for that question. Second, chances are good that your weaknesses are the things that stand in your way of happiness and success at work. In fact, your weaknesses are closely aligned with what you hate doing. Doing this exercise will help you stay clear on what you are not good at, and hopefully avoid those things in your next job. For example, if you are a "visionary" you are probably not good at the detail work. Taking a job that requires you to do a huge amount of documentation would not be a good fit for you.

Personal weaknesses:

Worksheet 24: My features and benefits

Do you know your own features and benefits? This worksheet is designed to capture yours, so that you can package yourself well when you are ready to write your resume, cover letter and other communication tools. Too often, people jump right in to writing their resumes, and miss some key experiences, training and awards that they have had.

Awards and recognition:

Training:

Notable skills:

Soft Skills:

Technical skills:

Industry experience:

Worksheet 25: My 30-second pitch

Tell Me About Yourself ... in 30 Seconds or Less

Defining what you want is the most important thing in your search for a new job. Developing a 30-second pitch is the **second most important thing**. Yes, it is more important than your resume. It should be fairly easy now that you've done some of the hardest work. Your 30-second pitch is what you tell people when you meet them and they ask, "What are you looking for?" or, "Tell me about yourself."

30-second pitch:

Sample Template for your 30-second pitch:
- "Hi, my name is _____."
- "I am a _____(something catchy and memorable if you can – a tagline)_____."
- "I am on the hunt for _____."
- "I would really appreciate your help (how they can help you get what you want).
- "In short, I bring (VERY high-level view of your background)."
- "Something unique about me is _____."

Worksheet 26: My marketing plan

You are now ready to tell the world what makes you great and ask for help getting it. A target marketing plan can help you do this. It will help you take your talents and newfound confidence to the streets.

In short, I am (your 30-second commercial inserted here):

Target positions / roles / job titles:

Sampling of target companies:

I would like to meet the following networking contacts:

Sample career accomplishments:

Thank you very much for your time and consideration. I appreciate any support or suggestions you can send my way!

Jane Doe

Worksheet 27: My resume

Are you ready? It's time to capture your background and expertise **as it relates to what you want** and **as it demonstrates your value-add** in the form of a resume. This worksheet will be a living document, getting updated as you go along in your job search and in your career. It is your tool for creating a resume that works. You will translate this worksheet into a final resume template you like, and that will work for your target market.

Professional summary / objective:

Functional expertise (example customer service, sales, leadership, etc.):

Industry experience:

Career highlights (look to your accomplishments on Worksheet 20):

Work experience (repeat this for each job and keep throughout career):

Company Name:

Company Address:

Manager name / contact information:

Start & End date:

Start date:_____End date:_____

Salary information:

Starting salary:_____Ending salary:_____

Benefit information: (vacation, medical, dental, vision, etc.)

Reason for leaving:

Title:

Duties:

Worksheet 28: My commitments to myself

Congratulations! You are now extremely well-prepared to go get the job you want – faster and easier! Do stop to celebrate and pat yourself on the back for a lot of work well-done.

Before you launch into your job hunt, it is a great idea to make some personal commitments. You have come this far because you care about the next job you take. You care about the life you live. So make some commitments to yourself in terms of what you are going to accomplish each day, and each week, to make this happen. You know best what your danger areas are. Own them. Make a commitment to yourself to overcome them so that you can get a job you'll love. Fast.

The following template is merely a suggestion. Make it your own. Yes, this is about you. Right now. If you are unemployed, then you need to make some big time commitments especially, unless you have a huge financial cushion and do not need or want a job anytime soon. If you are gainfully employed right now, and not in danger of losing your job, then you can make smaller time commitments to expanding your network and hunting for that next great job.

I am committing to the following:

I will work _____ hours per week on my job hunt.

I will ask for help.

I will not beat myself up during this process.

I will remember that I am very talented, and that I will be an asset to the right organization.

I will NOT take a job that _____.

If I lose sight of how great I am, I will call my champion(s) for support.

I will do something nice for myself once a week.

Signed: _____

Date: _____

Worksheet 29: My job hunt action plan

Note: *You are not allowed to beat yourself up during this process. If looking at the sample action plan (above) makes you short of breath, then push some items into week two. Set yourself up for success, but set yourself up for a push as well.*

How I will spend my time:

Networking: _____%
Online _____%

Week One:

Have [_____] review my resume for me

Have [_____] review my marketing summary

Make and order business cards

Start reaching out to my network and setting face to face appointments

Post my resume online selectively

Set up job agents online

Daily goals:

_____ phone calls per day

_____ personal connections per day (over the phone or e-mail; phone is ideal)

_____ in-person meeting (networking or interviews) per day

Daily schedule:

Congratulations!

We hope you find the job of your dreams very soon.

Please let us know how we can improve this book and worksheets so that we can help others. We are always striving to offer the best relevant job searching information.

www.arbez.com